How-To Paint Tractors & Trucks

Timothy Remus

Published by:
Wolfgang Publications Inc.
Stillwater, MN 55082
www.wolfpub.com

Legals

First published in 2008 by Wolfgang Publications Inc.,
PO Box 223, Stillwater MN 55082

The information in this book is true and complete to the best of our
knowledge. All recommendations are made without any guarantee
on the part of the author or publisher, who also disclaim any liability
incurred in connection with the use of this data or specific details.

We recognize that some words, model names and designations, for
example, mentioned herein are the property of the trademark holder.
We use them for identification purposes only. This is not an official
publication.

ISBN number: 1-929133-47-2
ISBN-13: 978-1-929133-47-5

Printed and bound in China.

How-To Paint Tractors & Trucks

Acknowledgements

If it takes a village to raise a child, it takes a lot of friends and hard working professionals to produce a good how-to book.

My thanks start with Bruce Bush and Greg Anderson, the two individuals who did the actual body and paint work – these are the guys who painted the tractor and truck, and allowed me access to their shops. They even wrote the captions for those particular chapters.

Most of the paint they sprayed came from Valspar, more specifically from two long-time Valspar reps, Jeff Edington and Bob Larson. Another hard working professional is John Ballard from Evercoat. John helped with the Rage side-bar and with the section on spray guns (John also works with DeVilbiss).

For help with media blasting I have to thank a hard working small businessman by the name of Curt at LNE Blasting in Harris, Minnesota. Troy Anderson is another small businessman working hard at his particular specialty, powder coating. Without Troy there would be no Chapter Nine. And without John from Redi-Strip there would be no side-bar on dip stripping as a way to remove all the old paint and rust without damaging the metal itself.

Tom Rad is a long time fixture in Minnesota's custom painting world. Though Tom spends most of his time painting custom motorcycles, he took an afternoon to show me the basics of setting up and adjusting a modern HVLP spray gun.

As always, I have to thank my team: Mary Lanz (my lovely and talented wife) for proof reading, Jacki Mitchell for layout, Richard Thompson for sales and Krista Leary for keeping the office running on an even keel.

Timothy Remus

Introduction

There is something special about an old tractor or truck. Call it mechanical simplicity, a certain honesty, a straightforward approach to the work at hand. These are work vehicles. No air conditioning and no fancy stereo. Just a torquey motor, a strong chassis and a simple body.

Whether it's a Case tractor or an old Dodge pickup truck, these machines deserve to be brought back to life. If not to work, at least to run under the sun as representatives from a simpler time.

To help you get organized and up to speed on the latest paint and products, the first three chapters cover: The Paint, The Shop, and The Gun. To help you understand the various steps involved in painting that old machinery we present two, start-to-finish paint jobs. Throughout the book a variety of interviews and side-bars bring to light the best way to use and mix filler, fix a dent without filler, and sandblast the panels.

The primer and paint materials available today are not only of very high quality, they are simpler than ever before. No longer do you need one primer for the bare metal, and another that will fill 80 grit scratches, followed by a separate sealer product. Today, you can buy one product that will do all three jobs. Which makes the whole operation simpler and less expensive.

The goal here isn't necessarily a perfect paint job. The goal is to help you keep that old machinery running and looking good. An old mechanic friend once said, "the best tune up you can give a car is a wash job." And by the same token, the best engine overhaul you can give an old truck or tractor is a paint job. A paint job, even a simple one, is a very cost-effective way to keep a piece of old machinery not only looking good, but relevant. A vehicle you can be proud of. A vehicle that deserves to be used and maintained.

Too many of our old treasures are left to rot in the sun. Our goal with this book is simple. To convince you to drag that old tractor or truck out of the barn or out of the grove, and give it a paint job. Do it with a brush and three gallons of oil base paint, or do it with a spray set up and the latest two-stage automotive grade paint. We don't care. No matter what you do, it will look better after than it did before.

Just do it.

Chapter One

The Paint

What's Inside the Can

To say modern paints have come a long way is a huge understatement. The latest coating technology means easier application of the paint, better durability of the finished product, and many new multi-use products that make the whole operation simpler and safer.

Any paint, be it an oil-based enamel, or high-tech urethane, is made up of three basic components: Resin, pigment and solvent, The resin is the backbone, it's what makes it what it is, and

A trip to the local Tractor Supply Store (shown) or hardware store will reveal a large selection of paint, much of it enamel. Most offer a hardener that can be used to increase the performance of the paint. Many of these paints are available in the original tractor colors.

provides the strength. Pigment is the color. The solvent (this is not the same as the reducer), is used to blend the components together. The solvent affects the way the paint lays out and dries. It's more than just a generic petroleum product. The solvents evaporate (or oxidize) into the atmosphere and are known in the paint industry as VOCs (volatile organic compounds) and are regulated to minimize their contribution to air pollution.

After the solvents evaporate and the paint dries you are left with the pigment and the resin.

The thinner, or reducer, is used to make the paint sprayable. Much of the reducer actually evaporates before the paint hits the surface. Which is why you don't want to leave the can sitting on the bench with the cap off.

In the good old days, there were three kinds of paint: lacquer, enamel and urethane. Today, there are really only two kinds of paint: enamel and urethane. Lacquer has fallen from favor for at least two reasons; a high VOC content, and durability that doesn't compare to high quality enamels and catalyzed urethanes.

Which leaves us with enamels and urethanes. Enamel paint can be used to paint everything from your house to your tractor. Enamel paints can be catalyzed with a hardener for greater durability, but even without the catalyst enamel

The Tractor & Implement Finish line from Valspar is available in most typical tractor colors, from Ford blue to John Deere green.

The same line of paint seen above is also available in spray cans.

It's important to match the primer to the paint, to ensure the two are compatible. Most primers recommend that you apply additional coats of primer, or the finish paint, with a certain window of time.

makes a good durable surface. Perhaps the greatest downside to enamel is the long dry times, which means more wet-time when dust can become trapped on the surface, and longer waits to apply additional coats of paint.

Urethane paint is synonymous with "automotive grade." In the world of factory paint, and custom paint, 99% of the paint is catalyzed urethane.

Enamel paints use a thinner to help make the paint sprayable, while urethanes use a reducer. No matter which paint company's urethane you use, the reducer is available in various grades or part numbers, each one designed to work within a certain temperature range.

If you use a hardener to improve the performance of an enamel paint, be sure it's a recommended product, and that you follow the safety recommendations when handling this material. This particular hardener is available in 4 different part numbers for use with projects of different sizes.

ENAMEL PAINTS

Tractor & Implement Enamel from Valspar is considered a heavy duty anti-rust paint. This enamel is designed from the very start for use on farm equipment and machinery. Anyone who is restoring an old tractor or combine will appreciate the fact that this paint is available in matching colors for most popular brands of tractors and machinery. The Tractor & Implement paint can be used on wood as well as metal and is non-toxic to any of the critters on the farm.

Unlike many modern paints, this product can be applied with an old-fashioned brush. Spray application can be used as well, though it requires thinning with VM&P Naptha.

Moving up the quality ladder, Restoration Tractor and Implement Finish is considered an automotive-quality enamel. This product can be purchased in a pre-mixed color that will match the color of nearly any American tractor. Unlike the Tractor & Implement Enamel, this enamel is designed for spray application only. This high quality enamel can be made even more durable through the use of the recommended hardener, which extends the life of both the gloss and the color. Be sure you handle the hardener with the necessary caution.

MODERN URETHANE

Urethane paint is technically an enamel, yet if offers very fast dry times and durability unmatched by any of the more typical enamel paints. Urethanes come in singe and two-stage. A single stage paint is just what it says, a product that you mix, reduce and spray – period. Though there may be a second coat there is no clearcoat used with a single-stage paint.

Two-stage urethanes, sometimes called base-coat/clearcoat paints, are paints that dry with a dull finish and are designed to be topcoated with clear, the product that provides gloss.

The Restoration product is available in all the standard tractor colors (no special mixing required), and uses a specific thinner to make the product thin enough to spray. This is a good product to use if you intend to show the tractor, as it duplicates the original finish.

Most paint companies offer mixing cups that make it easy to combine the paint with the correct proportion of thinner, or reducer, and activator (when used).

Urethane paints are available in two stage and single stage. This single stage paint requires no clearcoat, uses a reducer instead of a thinner, and an activator (or catalyst).

Basecoat/clearcoat paints were originally developed for the new metallic and pearl products used in the automobile industry. In the case of a truck where you want to use a metallic, you are better off to use a basecoat/clearcoat paint. Don't attempt a single stage high metallic paint unless you're an experienced painter.

What helps give urethanes their durability and high gloss is the catalyst. In the Valspar line the single-stage urethanes and the clearcoats that are part of the basecoat/clearcoat products, are both catalyzed. These catalyzed products are the standard of the industry and offer durability unmatched by any other paint product. Because of the toxicity of the catalyst, however, a full paint suit and fresh-air mask should be worn while painting and handling this material.

BASECOAT

Two of the three start-to-finish paint sequences offered farther along in the book were done with the 999 Series Zenith Z Base Valspar paint. This basecoat is designed to provide the color but not the gloss. Two or three medium coats are all that's required for good coverage, and the second and third coats go on in as little as ten minutes after the prior coat. These basecoats are not catalyzed, which means no fresh-air hood is required to protect the

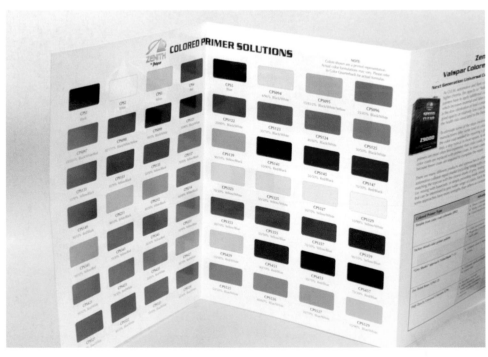

The trend in primer and sealers is toward tinting. By making the primer and sealer the same color as the topcoat, fewer coats are needed to get the correct color. This chart shows available colors for the Valspar primer.

painter during the application. All you need is a TC-23 type respirator, a paint suit, and gloves.

CLEARCOATS

Most paint companies offer a number of urethane clearcoats. From the Valspar line, the 4400 product is a good topcoat for the Z Base basecoat. The clear is always catalyzed, which means a fresh-air hood is recommended. These systems can be rented, or you can take the vehicle to a commercial shop with booth and all the correct safety equipment and have them apply the clear.

Because this is a tractor painting book, it's worth noting that at the shows some judges deduct points for a basecoat/clearcoat paint job as these were never available when the tractors were new.

WHERE TO BUY THE PAINT

Assuming for the moment that tractor painters will likely use enamel and that truck painters use urethane, let's consider where you might buy that perfect paint.

TRACTOR PAINT

No matter which brand of paint you buy, you have a choice as to where you make that purchase. You can buy a gallon of enamel at any hardware store. If what you want though is a gallon of enamel in the right color for your particular tractor, you likely need to find a store or chain of stores that specialize in

Some painters prefer a two stage paint like this Z Base from Valspar. The basecoat is the color, and each coat dries fast. The clearcoat provides the gloss and protects the basecoat.

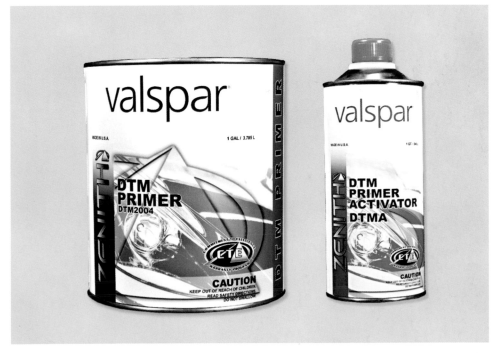

The DTM product is a good example of the new multi-task primer/sealer products that can be used as a primer and a sealer. The DTM is also tintable.

Epoxy primers typically bond tenaciously to the metal and provide a very durable foundation for the next layers of paint.

tractor parts and paint (this includes some hardware store chains). Remember too that not all pre-mixed paint is created equal. There were two "John Deere greens" used, for example, and some of the two-cylinder green is an accurate color and some is not.

TRUCK PAINT

A gallon of automotive grade paint generally requires a trip to the local NAPA store or paint jobber. When you make a stop at the local jobber, understand that most of these stores stay in business by serving the local body shops. Which means their typical buyer knows exactly what he or she needs and buys a lot of material in a week's time. You, on the other hand, with your endless questions, might be nothing more than a speed bump in that counter-person's day.

If urethane paint is what you need or want, then look for a store that serves individuals. A store that sells to street rodders and restorers is more likely to have the time and the attitude to answer questions.

When it comes to buying the right material for your project, a good counter person can be a great deal of help. If you're confused about which paint to buy, just ask them: "which paint would you use?"

What we think of as "thinner" comes in range of forms and brands. Be sure you use the correct product before adding it to a quality enamel product.

Q&A: Which Paint to Use

For help in choosing the right paint, we asked Kendra Fleck, the manager of the Tractor Supply Store in Inver Grove Heights, Minnesota, if she could walk us through some of the basics questions that any first time painter is likely to have.

Let's say I'm rookie painter, how do I know which paint to use and which one is best for my project?

As a rule of thumb, the better the paint, the more durable and more long lasting the finish will be. The question is: is this uncle John's old tractor and I want it perfectly restored, or is it just an old work tractor or daily-driver truck. To some extent the paint you use depends on the project.

There are a variety of enamels on the shelf, what is an appropriate use for these paints?

The least expensive materials are typically easy to use and easy to re-coat. As you get into more expensive products, like the two-parts, they are more durable but also more difficult apply and to re-coat. As they get into more expensive paint you need better tools and more thorough preparation.

What are the safety issues that should be considered when using a hardener?

Hardeners, or activators for two-part materials, make the paint more durable and longer lasting. They provide better gloss and better color retention. You should wear a fresh-air hood and a full painter's suit when mixing or spraying these materials. Remember though that no matter how good your personal protection is, you need air movement in the shop. Otherwise you're still standing in a fog of paint fumes.

If I want a pretty nice paint job with a spray gun, what do you recommend for paint.

You can either use our Restoration enamel, or a single stage urethane. If you are painting a tractor to go to a show, an enamel or single stage urethane is what you want to use. Judges are now deducting points for base/clear paint jobs because they never came from the factory that way.

What are the pros and cons of the base-coat/clearcoat paints?

Base/clear paints were developed for the new metallic and pearl products used in the automotive industry. If you want the truck to have a new metallic color you better use a base/clear paint. Don't attempt a single stage high-metallic paint with a single stage if you are not experienced.

Do I have to buy these paints from an auto parts store?

You can buy the enamels from either a chain like ours that specializes in tractor parts and paint, or a hardware store. Automotive paints, like the urethanes, will probably have to come from some kind of auto parts store.

Can I buy any standard tractor color in a pre-mixed paint?

At our stores you can buy all the common tractor colors in quarts and gallons. This would be our Restoration line. We have both of the John Deere colors for example, and our colors are very accurate. The nice thing about buying the paint already mixed is that as long as you don't open the can, and you keep the cover clean, the extra paint can be returned when the job is over. The other nice thing about our particular chain is that we buy a lot of paint so the prices are very competitive. If you're having paint mixed, like a urethane for example, ask the store to mix up a small quantity. Then take that home, spray it on some sheet metal and see if it matches.

What mistakes do people make when they buy paint?

They don't get the data sheets for the product, so it's harder to follow the directions and mixing ratios. The paints are always changing, so you need the current data sheet. I tell people to tack the data sheet up in the shop so it's right there for reference. And you do have to be accurate when you measure and use the products.

Chapter Two

The Shop

Make it Safe and Efficient

TEMPORARY OR PERMANENT

Whether you're painting equipment, tractors or old trucks, you need a place do the painting. An area that's relatively free of dust, where you can keep the temperature at about 70 degrees, where there's enough light so you can see what

you're doing and enough clean, dry air to run the spray gun without having to stop every ten minutes to let the compressor catch up.

You have to decide if this is going to be your only paint job, or if you intend to do more than

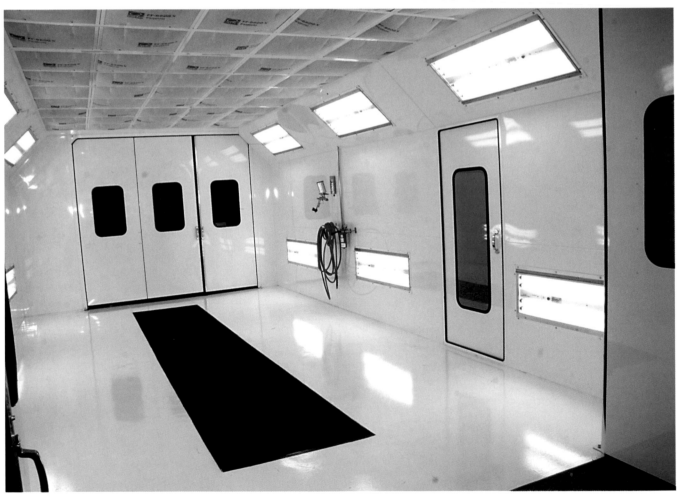

The Cadillac of spray booths, a new downdraft booth from Tecor. While the individual working in a small shop is unlikely to buy something so elaborate, the things that make this a great booth apply to any booth: good air movement, good lighting, dust and temperature control, a safe environment to work in.

one paint job. Is this paint-booth you're building going to be temporary or permanent?

THE AIR SUPPLY

You need a big enough compressor – period. Yes, it's the single most expensive item on the tools list, but without it you can't do a good paint job. We've all worked with compressors too small for the job. Waiting for the compressor to catch up means you can't "walk the car" or lay the paint in nice, long, uninterrupted passes. Compressors that work too hard create a lot of heat and are more likely to pass contaminants through to the spray gun (especially true of piston-style compressors).

Check the requirement for the spray gun you just purchased and add a fudge factor. We used to worry about horsepower, but anymore, having a five or eight horse compressor isn't enough, your gun and your equipment require a certain CFM (Cubic Feet Per Minute). When you shop for a compressor pay attention to the CFM, not the HP.

If this is a one time deal, or if you just don't have the budget for a good compressor, consider renting. Most big rental shops have compressors that can be rented for a day or a week.

A permanent booth will need permanent lines. Though there are glue-together PVC plastic lines, the old standard for feeding

This is a typical home-shop air compressor, and if you read the fine print, the CFM rating is only 7.0 at 40psi - which is probably not enough to run a modern spray gun.

At Northern Tool and Equipment they sell a whole range of professional quality compressors. Don't use horsepower as a means of judging the capacity of a compressor. Read the tags and be sure you have enough CFM to run your spray gun and the power tools in the shop.

air to the booth is galvanized of at least one-half inch inside diameter. New on the scene is an air distribution system based on nylon tubing and easily assembled fitting and distribution manifolds called RapidAir from Garage Toys. These lines can be used inside or out, as exposed run of pipe or hidden behind the sheet rock.

Regardless which air distribution system you install, a shut off both at the compressor and each drop point is a great convenience. Remember, the longer the lines the more air you loose along the way, almost like voltage drop in an electrical circuit. Note the chart on page 21. If it's a long way from the compressor to the booth you need to use larger diameter piping.

Professional filtering systems combine a typical water bowl with a filter, and desiccant dryers. Similar, though less complex, filtering systems are available for small shops for well under a hundred dollars.

FILTERS AND WATER SEPARATORS

The air passing through the gun must be absolutely clean and free of moisture. Which means you need more than just a simple water trap at the compressor. The air leaving the compressor is hot so moisture in the air is in suspension. As the air gets farther away from the compressor and cools, that's when the moisture will turn to liquid drops that make the spray gun spit. So buy at least a good water separator and put it as close to the spray gun as you can. Don't forget to drain the compressor tank on a regular basis. If this is a permanent booth think about a dedicated in-line filter designed for a spray booth. Many of the problems that crop up in a paint job can be traced to dirty air or air contaminated with moisture.

The flexible line in the booth itself should be 3/8 inch, and only as long as is required to reach the corners of the booth. Extra hose causes additional pressure drop, and if you have a huge tangle of air hose laying on the cold floor any moisture is more likely to condense into water drops that are carried to the gun.

A BOOTH WITH AIR MOVEMENT

Clean air means not only the air coming out of the spray gun, but the air in the booth. Ideally you want to filter the air coming into the booth so it's free of dust and contaminants. Remember that paint is not compatible with any products that contain silicone. Keep the area "upwind" from the booth free of products that might contaminate a paint job.

If you plan to paint in the barn or garage you have to remember that the most important thing is air movement. If you don't move enough air the solvent doesn't leave the paint. The end result is solvent pop or gloss die back. Air movement is essential, you need a good exhaust fan and a filter on the air leaving the booth so that you're not putting contaminates onto your neighbor's land or into the air. They have what they call arresting filters that grab the over-spray and catch it before it gets outside.

The paint mist in the booth is flammable, so you don't want to pull it out of the shop with just any old fan. You want an explosion-proof fan. This means the motor is contained, so mist cannot be exposed to sparks within the motor housing. A little more money, but well worth it for peace of mind.

You can use sheets of poly to create a paint booth, but only for a single paint job. Because once the plastic has paint on it, the dried paint will flake off and create dirt that will find its way into the next paint job. A better idea is to build something with pre-made panels. Many of these come with a glossy, easy-to-clean surface and can be held in place with plastic "rivets." For a spray booth at home in one stall, that stuff is not too expensive and it holds up really well. Anything you use is alright as long as you paint it first so it holds the dirt down and you can clean the walls. Remember that a wet floor helps to trap and hold down the dust during the actual painting.

HEAT

Even if you live in a southern state, you're likely to need heat in the shop. When it comes to heat, there are two important points worth considering. One, the booth and shop are filled with flammable materials. Two, you can't paint, especially with modern catalyzed paints, in much less than 70 degrees. Not only does the booth need to be 70 when you paint, it needs to stay at 70

Though this booth with curtains instead of hard walls is meant as a professional prep station, it could easily serve as a template for a home-based paint booth. The curtains are available separately from Tecor.

Fluorescent lights provide nice even illumination in this professional booth. Be sure the lights you use are daylight-balanced, put the fixture itself behind a piece of glass or plexiglass - and keep the light switch outside the booth.

The intake filters in this downdraft booth are called dispersal type, as they tend to disperse the air evenly throughout the upper air plenum so it doesn't all blow down though one small area.

while the paint cures. If the booth doesn't stay at about 70 you have the same trouble with trapped solvents that you do with insufficient air movement.

Because the paints are flammable, not to mention gas in the gas tank, the idea of using an old barrel stove or home made wood burner is out of the question. You don't want a gas unit with open flame or a pilot light in the booth. Even a gas unit that hangs from the ceiling needs to be kept away from the paint mist.

Electric heat is one option, hot water or in-floor heat provide a more expensive, but otherwise ideal, solution. Small gas heaters with sealed combustion chambers might work well, though most have a fan that might create dust. Think carefully before deciding which is the best way to heat that new booth.

FIRE EXTINGUISHES

You always need fire extinguishers, placed by your exits. They have to be on the wall not sitting on the floor. You want them where it's easy to grab 'em. Familiarize yourself with their use so it's easy to just point it at the fire and pull the trigger if you ever do have a fire. They make powdered ones and they make the CO_2 fire extinguishers. The Halon-style are the cleanest because there is no mess, but you can't use them in a closed space because they deplete the oxygen.

Overspray exits the downdraft booth through the series 55 filters built into the floor.

Professional Spray Booths

Though most amateur painters aren't going to buy an expensive paint booth worth $50,000 or $60,000, we all need some kind of a "booth" so we can control the air movement, temperature and the amount of dust in the area where we intend to do the painting.

For a little insight into how the professionals make booths, and what the amateurs can learn from the pros, we spent an afternoon at Tecor, in Burnsville, Minnesota.

THE BEST BOOTH

In a commercial environment the down draft booth is considered the best, mostly because it gets rid of overspray quicker than a cross flow booth. The booth doesn't drag the overspray all the way across the vehicle so there is less chance to get dry spray paint on the car or truck. As the air moves from the ceiling to the floor an envelope of air is formed around the car, and the overspray is quickly pushed or pulled to the floor and out of the booth.

At Tecor they also make a semi-downdraft booth, where the air enters through the ceiling but then exits either to one of the walls, or to air plenums along the floor. The design offers many of the advantages of the downdraft booth without the need to bust up the floor and install the grating and a path for the air to exit under the car.

Least expensive is the older cross-draft style booth where the air simply enters at one end and exits at the other. And it is this style that is easiest to construct if you're building your own booth.

FANS THAT PUSH OR PULL

The downdraft booths at Tecor have fans that push air through the booth, rather then try to suck the fumes out on the exhaust side. The demonstration booth at Tecor uses a fan on the roof to push air into the booth through the filters in the ceiling. That same air travels through the grates in the floor, through the exit filters and back out into the environment. The intake filters eliminate the dust in the incoming air, and the exhaust filters collect the overspray so what exits the booth is clean air not a mist of paint overspray.

As Kurt Chellberg from Tecor, explained, "most of our booths have positive pressure inside, so if there's a crack in the door the air from the booth leaks out into the shop. With a more typical booth the pressure is negative so a crack in the door will suck dust into the booth from the outside." Placing the fan on the intake side of the booth has an added advantage, the fan blades and motor are not in the path of the flammable exhaust fumes so there is no worry about the need for explosion proof motors and spark-resistant fans.

The prep station uses what's called a semi-downdraft design. Incoming air enters through the filters in the ceiling and then exits through the filter in the back wall.

A variety of intake and exhaust filters are available for your spray booth. Most come in a large roll, or panels like those shown here, which can slip into fabricated doors or wall sections in the booth.

A SOURCE OF LIGHT

Everyone uses fluorescent lighting, but the typical fluorescent light isn't a full-spectrum light. If you use the regular cheap fluorescent bulbs from the hardware store the color in the booth isn't accurate so it's hard to judge the color of your paint job. If you're just painting John Deere green as it comes out of the can, it might not matter. If you want something more accurate, full spectrum lights are available from companies like ParaLite, or you can buy "daylight" fluorescent tubes for about twice what the cheap ones cost at your local Menards or Hardware Hank.

The other issue that comes up here is the same one that arises when fans are discussed. You can't have sparks in the booth. And though lights rated as "explosion proof" are available they tend to be expensive. If you check out the booth at the local body shop you're likely to see lights set behind glass. If your booth is semi-permanent you want to cut holes in the walls, glue glass or lexan to the hole and then mount the light outside the glass. And always put the switch for the light outside the booth. There are some very helpful web sites for anyone putting together a booth. Just Google: explosion-proof fans, or spray booth, or spray booth equipment.

These Series 55 exhaust filters, made from fiberglass, feature a progressive weave - the fiber weave gets tighter toward the "back" of the filter. Otherwise, all the material catches on the front surface and the filter loads up too quickly.

PROTECT YOURSELF

For spraying primer and non-catalyzed basecoats you need to protect your lungs with a TC-23 style of mask with cartridges intended for use in a body shop environment. These masks are only as good as the the seal around your nose and mouth, so be sure your beard or mustache isn't keeping the mask from sealing around your face.

When using today's catalyzed paints a regular TC-23 style face mask is not adequate. Having a hood that's supplying you with fresh air through a special filter is the ideal set up and they're not that costly.

The air-supplied respirator uses specially filtered air from your compressor, or from its own compressor, to supply pressurized breathable air for the air hood. Because the air is constantly flowing through the hood, there's very little chance for paint fumes to seep in where you're going to breath them.

You have to think about where the compressor is picking up the air for the mask. You don't want the small compressor feeding the hood to draw in contaminated air or you've defeated the whole purpose of the air-supply hood.

When spraying even non-catalyzed paints and primers in an area with poor air flow it's a good idea to use a full air-sup-

Pressure Loss with 100 psi Inlet Pressure

	35' HOSE		50' HOSE	
	15 CFM	25 CFM	15 CFM	25 CFM
1/4" ID	35 psi	87 psi	50 psi	*
5/16" ID	12.6 psi	31.5 psi	18 psi	45 psi
3/8" ID	4.2 psi	10.5 psi	6 psi	15 psi

Here's an example of the kinds of pressure drop you will experience when using hoses of too small an inside diameter.

Minimum Pipe Size Recommendations

Compressor Size	Compressor Capacity	Main Air Line	Min. Pipe Diameter
1-1/2 & 2 HP	6 to 9 CFM	Over 50 ft.	3/4"
3 & 5 HP	12 to 20 CFM	Up to 200 ft.	3/4"
		Over 200 ft.	1"
5 to 10 HP	2 to 40 CFM	Up to 100 ft.	3/4"
		100 to 200 ft.	1-1/4"
		Over 200 ft.	1-1/4"
10 to 15 HP	40 to 60 CFM	Up to 100 ft.	1"
		100 to 200 ft.	1-1/4"
		Over 200 ft.	1-1/2"

* Under no circumstances are we advising that correct air line piping reduces contaminants so much that you do not need a filtering system. A point of use filter is still strongly recommended.

The bigger the compressor, and the longer the main feed line, the bigger the pipe diameter needs to be. DeVilbiss

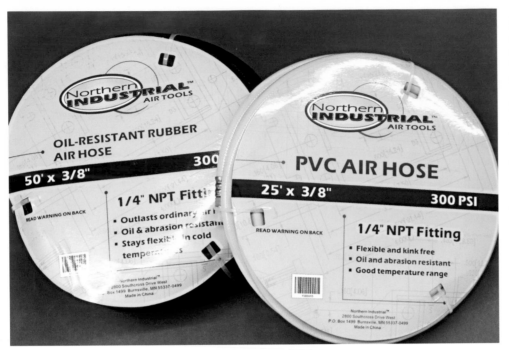

Hoses used to feed the spray gun need to be at least 3/8 inch inside diameter - and not any longer than needed, note the nearby chart.

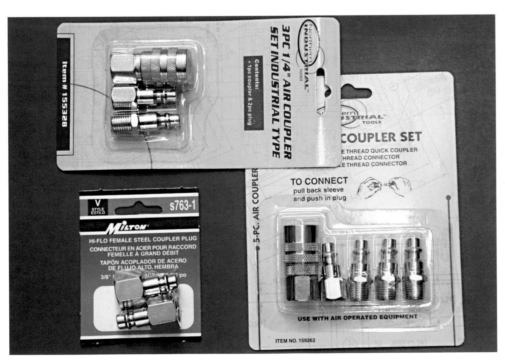

Try to avoid the 1/4 inch couplers. Coupler sets with a larger I.D. are available, though they may be harder to find.

ply hood. Take the best care possible of your lungs – they are irreplaceable.

A Painter's Suit

Much of the lint and dirt that ends up in your paint job comes not from the air in the booth but from your clothing, your T-shirt or flannel shirt. A good painter's suit prevents the lint on your clothes from finding their way into the paint job.

Multiple points of entry

Protecting your lungs isn't always enough. Paint fumes and solvent residues can find their way into your body through the mucous membranes around your eyes, which is why some painters wear goggles or a full mask, and also another reason why you need air movement in the booth. Solvents and thinners are an often overlooked safety hazard in the shop. Many of us see them as benign and may even use them to wash paint off our hands. This is not a good idea. Solvents are highly toxic and should never be used to wash up and never handled without gloves.

Storage and Disposal

Because most of these materials are flammable, you want to store the paints, thinners and reducers in metal cabinets away from flames and sources of heat. Neatness counts here. Not only are these materials flammable, they're toxic as well so you have to keep everything covered and away from kids and animals.

No matter how carefully you plan, there are going to be leftover materials. And though it's tempting to just dump a small amount of paint out behind the garage, small amounts add up and soon the material finds its way to the water table.

You could also ask your buddy at the body shop to let you add your wastes to his, for pickup by the licensed disposal company that picks up at any commercial operation. Considering, however, that the body shop pays by volume and is responsible for all the wastes they generate, this might not be as easy as it sounds.

A better idea is to contact the Local Environmental Office. Usually a county function (in some cases the office is run by the city or township), nearly every community in the USA has a Local Environmental Office. Paint materials are considered HHW (Household Hazardous Wastes) and the Local Environmental Office will be able to direct you to the closest HHW collection site or provide a local information phone number. So don't let the stuff accumulate in the back corner of the garage. When the job is over, take all the leftover materials (preferably in their original containers) to the HHW collection site.

Save your lungs. Always wear a TC-23 type respirator, with cartridges approved for automotive paint, when doing any kind of painting. Some professionals use this style of respirator, instead of a simple dust mask, when sanding. The cartridges have a finite life, so keep the mask in a coffee can or heavy zip lock bag.

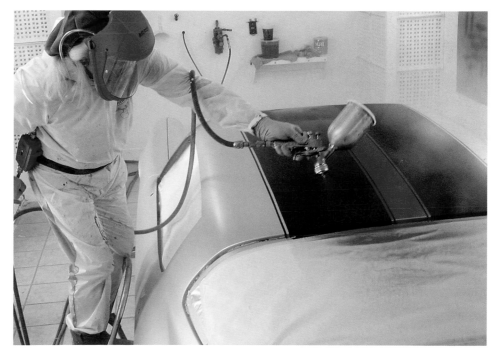

A fresh air hood provides the painter with pure air under pressure so no paint or fumes can be absorbed by the lungs or the mucous membranes around the eyes.

Chapter Three

The Gun

Buying and Using

A LITTLE HISTORY

The first spray gun was invented by a man named DeVilbiss during the American Civil War. The goal was not to atomize paint, but rather to atomize and spray disinfectants in the hospitals of the period. Eventually someone discovered that the same technology could be used to break liquid paint up into small droplets which were then carried by the air stream onto the house or machinery being painted. The key then, and now, is to fully atomize the paint, to break it up into very small droplets spread evenly though the "fan"

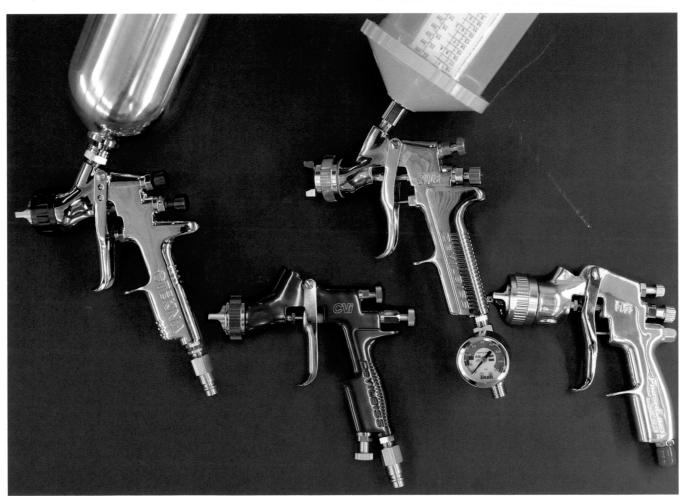

Guns come in every style and price range imaginable. On the right is an inexpensive HVLP gun from DeVilbiss, while in the center are two of their mid-priced models. On the far left is a Tekna, a premium gun designed to complete with the best that Europe has to offer.

of paint. At painting seminars the instructors talk about painting "with b-bs instead of bowling balls."

Designers and manufacturers soon discovered that more air meant better atomization, so the pressures went up, but the percentage of paint that actually stayed on the object being painted began to go down. At high pressures of forty psi or more, some of the paint never even makes it to the object, while a high percentage hits the surface with such force that it bounces off. A new term entered the vocabulary of paint gun designers: transfer efficiency. When measured carefully they discovered that as little as twenty five percent of the paint actually made it from the paint cup onto the car. The rest, along with the solvents mixed with the paint, went up into the air.

Inexpensive siphon-feed guns are available from a variety of sources.

The CVi is a quality, value-priced HVLP gun. Available fluid tips include 1.0, 1.2, 1.3 and 1.4mm.

As mentioned elsewhere, paint solvents are considered volatile organic compounds which contribute to air pollution. To reduce the amount of VOCs going up into the air, states like California began to insist that body shops and other paint facilities reduce the amount of VOCs entering the atmosphere.

Gun Types

Spray guns can be broken down into three types, with variations of course. Most older, traditional guns are siphon type, with the paint cup located under the gun. Air moving through the gun pulls the paint up from the cup where it mixes with the air stream. Though this design makes for a gun with a good feel and good balance, most of these are not HVLP designs.

Inside a quality spray gun: here we have a blow up of a new CVi gun.

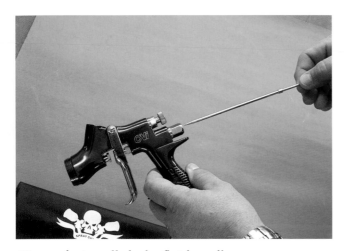

First to be installed, the fluid needle.

Next, John installs the adjustment knob for the needle.

Gravity feed guns take their name from the fact that gravity is used to feed the paint from the paint cup, which is located above the gun itself, to the air stream. Most new HVLP designs are gravity feed, and with the use of the plastic cup liners these guns can be used in nearly any position, even upside down. The cup liners mean clean up is easy and requires less solvent.

Pressure feed guns have no paint cup in the conventional sense. Instead, paint under pressure is fed to the gun through a hose. No longer are you limited to one quart of material, which is nice for industrial painting applications.

NEW GUNS

In order to increase the amount of paint that actually hits the surface being painted, and reduce the loses of both paint and solvent to the atmosphere, companies like DeVilbiss, Binks, Sharp and many more began to introduce guns designed to work at a lower pressure. By increasing the volume while reducing the pressure the designers were able to design guns that would atomize the paint and increase the transfer efficiency enormously.

Though the learning curve was steep for both manufacturers and users, today we have high quality HVLP guns available from a variety of sources that do a great job of both atomizing paint and meeting all the current regulations, which stipulate no more than 10 psi at the air cap.

While this might all seem like another case of unnecessary regulation, the story has a silver lining for anyone who buys his or her own paint. The increased transfer efficiency means simply that a gallon of paint will cover roughly three times as much surface as it would have twenty or more years ago. Put another way, you need less than half as much paint, and reducer, if you use a good HVLP gun. If you look at the cost of a gallon of high quality paint, you soon realize that the HVLP gun will pay for itself pretty quickly.

The other benefit of HVLP guns is the reduction in overspray and mist in the booth. If more of the paint is actually getting to the tractor or truck you're spraying, that means there's less wasted paint in the air. Which means less paint and solvent for you to breathe or absorb through your skin and mucous membranes – this is especially important in homemade paint booths which seldom have the air movement of a good commercial booth.

How Spray Guns Work

Nearly all current spray guns, whether HVLP or not, operate on the same principle. Essentially, air passing through the spray gun mixes with liquid paint as both exit the gun at the air cap. A two-stage trigger controls both the air and the paint, pulling the trigger back part way allows air to pass through the gun, while pulling it back farther adds paint to the air already passing through the gun. This feature allows a painter to apply paint across a panel, stop the flow of paint (but leave the air on) at the end of a panel and smoothly resume the flow of paint at the other of the panel as he starts the next pass.

Paint and air leave the gun at the air cap and immediately begin to mix. Breaking the paint into tiny particles, or atomizing it, occurs in two or three stages, starting at the point where the paint leaves the gun surrounded by a column of air. Additional air leaves the gun from small ports in the air cap. The third stage of atomization is provided by the outboard air ports in the "horns" of the air cap. These ports shape the column of paint into the familiar fan and provide a third level of atomization.

Most guns have two adjustments: air to the horns which affects the size and shape of the fan, and the material control, which limits the movement of the trigger and thus the needle. In addition, an increasing number of painters put an air-adjusting valve with pressure gauge on the bottom of the gun where the air hose is connected, even though manufacturers recommend against any valve the restricts the air flow to the gun.

The instructional material that comes with your new gun will include an air pressure recommendation. This recommendation is the right amount of air to feed that gun. Ideally the factory suggested pressure will provide the best pattern.

continued, page 30

The fluid tip is next. Each fluid tip is matched to a specific needle. If you change one you have to change the other.

The handy dandy wrench, the one that comes with the gun, is used to tighten up the fluid tip.

The key to gun longevity is to keep it clean. A kit like this one is available anywhere they sell spray guns.

Q&A: John Ballard

John Ballard is a hard working professional. A man who sells and supports both DeVilbiss spray equipment and Evercoat fillers and putties. When John isn't selling the equipment, he's using it in his own shop to restore the tractors that belong to him and his father in law, Bob Wolff.

For a non professional painter, do I need two guns, one for primer and one for everything else? And how much do I have to spend?

I have a package of two DeVilbiss HVLP guns with three tips for $140.00. That's a pretty good starting set up and it's not too expensive.

What about the tips, how does a person choose the right tip?

The paint manufacture will give you a recommendation. As a rule of thumb, primer requires a 1.8mm tip, 1.5 for color and 1.3 for clear.

What's HVLP and what are the advantages?

HVLP means high volume low pressure. The gun uses a high volume of air instead of high pressure to atomize and carry the paint. They have very high transfer efficiencies, meaning they put a high percentage of the paint on the vehicle. Which means you need to buy less paint, you create less of a mess in the shop, and there's less crap in the air for you to breathe.

What are the advantages of buying a brand name gun instead of a cheap gun from a discount store?

A good gun probably has a better pattern. And some of the import guns are not rebuildable. They are throw away guns. If you drop it, or the parts get worn, or you don't clean it well enough and you need to replace some parts, you can't. There are no parts available. The better guns are also more efficient, they will require a lower CFM at the input in order to achieve a given pressure and CFM output.

What are the typical problems that first-time painters encounter when they set out to paint an old truck or a tractor or whatever?

First-Timers don't spend enough time prepping the vehicle. They end up with lint and junk in the paint. This comes from contaminants in the line and debris on the floor. These painters don't have the filters and water separators that a professional shop does. It's important to clean everything, wipe off all contaminants and use masking paper to seal off areas you don't want painted. I tell them to use a desiccant snake and some Whirlwind filters. None of these products are expensive. The filters are only six or eight bucks each. The snake will help to catch moisture and

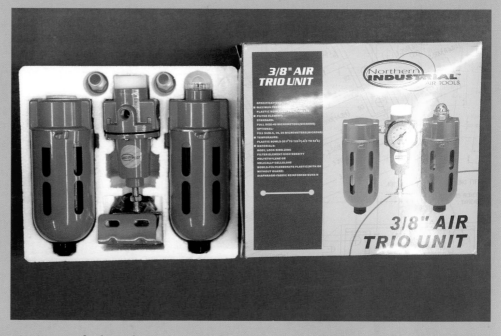

A variety of relatively inexpensive filter units are available, like this filter/drier combination with filters that go all the way down to 10 microns.

oil that gets past the standard water trap, and the filters will catch everything else. Keep the air clean.

How do I set up a new gun to start?

There are probably three adjustments on the gun. On the bottom is pressure in the gun, you

From DeVilbiss comes this nifty little in-line "tell-tale" that indicates excessive moisture in the air supply.

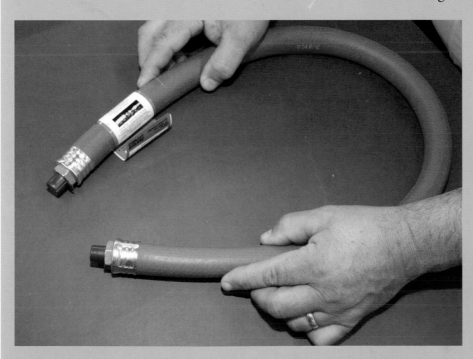

Sometimes call a "snake," what looks like an oversize hose is actually a hose from DeVilbiss filled with desiccant to dry the air as it passes through on its way to the spray gun.

want that all the way open. Top is the flow adjustment and you want this one all the way open. Last is the trigger adjustment, I tell people to depress the trigger all the way, then turn in the trig adjustment until you can feel the pressure on the trigger (you still have it pulled all the way), then release the trigger and go one more turn. You are now ready to start spraying.

How about compressor, how much compressor do I need?

You need at least a five-horse model with an 80 gallon tank, you probably have a good one for the air tools already.

What are the most common mistakes that new painters make in terms of buying and using a gun?

They don't keep them clean. You should pull the tip, nozzle and needle out each time. Remember, solvent by itself won't get them clean, you need a toothbrush or other bristle brush. Most paint has a 30 to 40 minute pot life, you have 40 minutes to get the paint on the car and the gun clean. If you let the paint set up in the gun you have a serious problem.

Any other words of advice?

Don't use anything that restricts the amount of air that gets to the gun, that includes cheater valves and hoses with too small an internal diameter.

It's a good idea to check the pressure at the gun, with the trigger pulled, so you know what that is and whether or not you're using the gun the way the manufacturer recommends.

You have to remember to keep the gun 90 degrees to the surface, overlap the spray pattern by 50%, as you paint, and move around the vehicle, a lot of people don't.

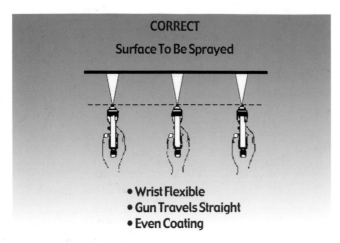

CORRECT

Surface To Be Sprayed

- Wrist Flexible
- Gun Travels Straight
- Even Coating

One of the keys to a good paint job is good gun handling. You have to keep the distance between the panel and gun and the...

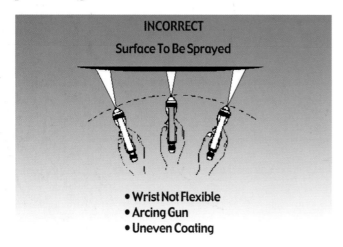

INCORRECT

Surface To Be Sprayed

- Wrist Not Flexible
- Arcing Gun
- Uneven Coating

...angle of the gun itself consistent. With long panels professionals "walk" the panel from one end to the other at a constant speed without stopping.

There are two adjustments on a typical gun, an upper adjustment for air to the air cap (the horns) and a lower material or trigger adjustment.

In terms of the care and feeding of your spray gun, the best advice can be summed up in three words: keep it clean.

GUIDELINES AND TIPS

Some people think HVLP – High Volume Low Pressure – means these guns put out a high volume of paint. Yes, they do have great transfer efficiency but the volume being referred to is the much larger volume of air required to operate the gun.

You need a good compressor to run any air gun, but this is especially true with an HVLP gun. Remember too that an enormous compressor won't do any good unless the connections between the compressor and gun have enough capacity.

The airlines in the booth should be 3/8 inch ID rather than 5/16 inch. The same applies to the fittings. Most quick couplers have a small ID and tend to limit air delivery to the gun. So pick good connectors and don't put any more in the line that is really necessary. The flexible hose should only be as long as necessary to reach all parts of whatever you're painting, to avoid loosing pressure and volume as the air passes through a too-long hose.

THE INITIAL SET UP

We spent part of an afternoon in the booth with Tom Rad, local custom painter, while he walked us through the basic adjustments on a typical HVLP gun and how to set those adjustments for the initial set up.

"This DeVilbiss gun uses two knobs on the back of the gun, the upper knob controls the size of the fan," explains Tom. "to start with you want this adjustment all the way open. The other adjustment is the fluid adjustment. I like to bottom out this adjustment and then back off three turns. This actually limits the movement of the trigger. And the other important part of set up is the pressure at the gun with the trigger pulled. The gun manufacturer provides a guideline, and there's another recommendation with the Material Data Sheet. Mostly the recommendations are between 29 and 35 psi."

Gun Adjustment & Spray Patterns

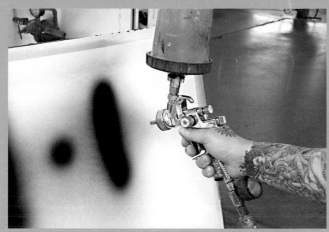

Before pointing that gun at the panel for the first time, it's a good idea to do a little test drive.

Here you can see a lop-sided pattern...

Tom Rad uses his hand as a guide, this is about how far you want the gun from the surface.

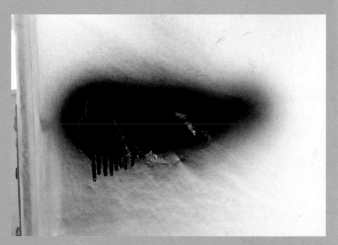

...which becomes more obvious with the horizontal pattern. This is likely caused by a dirty air cap.

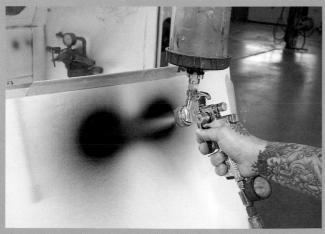

What can go wrong: too much air pressure at the gun will split the pattern as shown. Flaws like this are more obvious with the air cap turned ninety degrees.

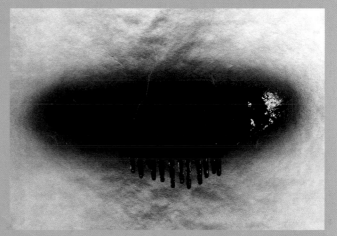

This is a pretty good pattern, with more paint in the center. Tom intentionally put the paint on too heavy so any excess could be easily seen.

Chapter Four

Metal Preparation

Sanding and Blasting

You can't put paint on rusty metal or old flaking paint and expect it to either look good or stay in place. Like a new house, a new paint job must be built on a solid foundation. No one would do a major renovation on an old barn if one foundation wall is sagging or full of cracks.

In a perfect world, an old truck or tractor would be stripped to its birthday suit before the new paint is applied. This is especially important when the vehicle in question is fifty or more

Sand or media blasting is a good way to remove paint and can be used without disassembly, but you have to be very careful to tape and seal off any openings so no abrasives find their way into the engine or various components.

years old and may have been painted many times.

When Bruce Bush painted the truck seen in Chapter Eight, he stripped part of it down to bare metal and in other areas he just took off the old flat black paint and sanded part way through the underlying paint. At the time, Bruce explained that, "how much paint you take off depends on the situation, you have to at least get down to some good solid stable paint, before you start building the new paint job." Anyone who plans to take off all or part of the old paint needs to consider a number of options for paint removal.

BLASTING

Sand blasting has long been used to remove paint but the method comes with one big drawback. As Greg Anderson points out in Chapter Seven, "sand blasting creates heat, you have to be sure the operator knows how to sand blast sheet metal without warping the metal." Some painters go so far as to recommend that sand blasting never be used on sheet metal. The key seems to be an experienced operator who knows enough to hold the nozzle at an angle to the sheet metal, turn down the pressure and keep the nozzle moving across the surface. Obviously, sand blasting

continued, page 37

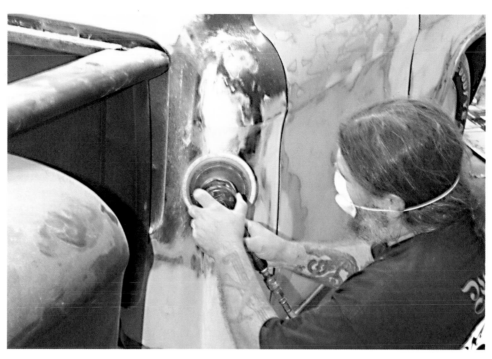

A DA (dual-action) sander is a good way to take off paint without damaging the underlying metal. If the paint is thick however, or the panels are large, this process can be very time consuming.

You can sandblast sheet metal, but the tip must be kept at an angle to the metal so the sand doesn't hit the steel straight on, which produces heat and can warp the metal. In other words, this requires an experienced operator.

Media Blasting at LNE

The plastic media comes in large barrels, and Curt grinds the raw plastic to the size shown here for the actual blasting.

The test object: a trunk lid off a small car. Nice graphics.

There are a number of ways to get the paint off those old body panels, and one of the more popular of late is media blasting. The process is similar to sandblasting, except that instead of sand, a plastic media is shot at the surface with high pressure air and used to take off the paint.

Curt, Peltier from LNE Blasting, in Harris, MN says that the best part of media blasting is the fact that there is no warpage, "it's not like sand blasting," explains Curt. "there's no friction and thus no heat, so you can blast sheet metal without any damage. I can even blast parts with the chrome still attached, and it won't hurt the chrome, and it doesn't hurt the window glass either, for that matter."

The media is plastic, and Curt says it comes in a raw condition, "and then I grind it into finer particles that work well for the type of work that I do." The material can be used up to six times, before it gets just too small to do any cutting.

The work Curt does includes everything from fenders to complete cars,

Media Blasting at LNE

and tractors. "When I blast the paint off a fender, I often find filler," explains Curt, "and I can either blast it all out or I can leave it, depending on what the customer wants."

In terms of preparing the metal for media blasting, "there's only really one thing people should do," says Curt. "They should clean off any heavy accumulations of grease. Otherwise I just push the grease around as I try to blast the parts, or I have to stop and clean it myself."

Q&A WITH CURT AT LNE BLASTING

Curt, how long have you owned LNE?

This is my third year as owner, but I've worked in the industry forever.

What's the biggest advantage of media blasting as compared to other types of blasting?

Does not warp the metal, made for sheet metal, no heat no friction.

You buy the plastic media in bulk?

Yes. When I buy it the individual pieces are

The stream of small plastic bits takes the paint, even multiple layers, off quickly and without any damage to the metal.

The finished trunk lid about ten minutes later. Ready for the first coat of primer.

35

Media Blasting at LNE

The fenders shown here have been media blasted. Note the remaining filler. "I can either leave the filler or blast it all out, it's up to the customer."

Media blasting projects include everything from individual panels to complete bodies with the chassis.

bigger than I want. So I can grind them to the size that's best suited to my needs.

Can the media be used more than once?

Yes, I use it up to six times, after that it's too small to be effective.

What about things like filler that you find under the paint, do you leave that or take it out?

I can do it either way. Sometimes with a restoration shop they want it left alone so they can show the owner the amount of work that still needs to be done. Other people will want the metal stripped totally bare. It all depends on the project.

How long does it take to blast off a typical part?

Depends of course on the size of the object and the paint, a typical trunk like the one we did is probably ten minutes of actual blasting.

You must have one hell of a compressor. How big is the compressor you use?

I use a 50 horse compressor.

What do you use to protect your body and protect yourself from breathing the dust?

I use a hood with a fresh air system. The hood is pressurized so I don't breath any of the dust.

works great for heavy chassis parts where warpage is not a problem.

If sand blasting seems overly aggressive and creates too much heat, consider one of the various media blasting methods. Media blasting uses something other than sand to remove the paint. Some shops use plastic media while others use soda or even peanut shells. The idea is to take off the paint with a material that's less aggressive than sand, one that is less prone to creating too much heat. For more on these less-aggressive blasting methods, check out the nearby side-bar on media blasting.

If blasting in one form or another seems the way to go, nearly any metro area will have a sand blasting operation. Check with local restoration shops to find out if a particular shop can be trusted with sheet metal. Media blasting has become more popular in the past ten or fifteen years, and these shops are relatively easy to find.

For hardcore do-it-yourselfers, home based kits for both sand and media blasting can be found in many tool catalogs, like Eastwood, and also available at various web sites. You can also find supplies, from bags of baking soda to 60-grit aluminum oxide at the same locations

One big plus to the idea of blasting is the fact that the resulting surface is very paint-friendly. The texture left by the sand or media is one that gives the paint a surface that's easy to hang on to. The other really nice thing about blasting is the way the nozzle can be worked up

continued, page 41

What we call "sand" comes in a huge variety of materials and sizes. Some of these aren't sand at all.

For the true do-it-yourselfer, there are a variety of strippers out there, some more toxic than others. Even in the best of situations, this is a messy operation that looks a lot like hard work.

Redi-Strip

Stripping paint is almost never easy. Whether you blast it, strip it or sand it, getting those many layers of paint off involves a lot of plain old work. Now imagine a process that strips all the paint off the sheet metal for that old tractor without any elbow grease. A process that will strip the paint off an entire car body or truck cab without any sanding or blasting. A perfect striping process that will eliminate the rust without any damage to the good metal.

At Redi-Strip, they have perfected the process described above. Everyday they dip fenders, hoods and complete bodies in the magical solutions. And each component, each complete body, emerges from the tank minus paint and minus rust.

PAINT STRIPPING

Paint removal is step number one. The parts or the complete body are immersed in a heated tank filled with an alkaline solution. After 24 hours they inspect the part, and likely drop it back into the solution for another 24 hours. Because it's a liquid doing the work, paint is removed from creases and hard-to-reach spots that a blasting operation could never reach.

RUST

The rust removal part of the program is an electrolytic process, similar in the essentials to the way in which a part is chrome plated, with one important difference. When a part is chrome plated, a source of DC electricity is used to entice the nickel or the chrome to adhere and bond with the bumper or carbure-tor. In the de-rusting tank,

the same principle is applied, though the polarity is reversed – the parts being stripped form the cathode or negative terminal. Iron oxide, rust, is pulled from the body, molecule by molecule. Like a heavy build up of paint, a heavy build up of rust takes a while to be stripped off.

Though the focus here is on bodies and body panels, heavy components like frames can be dipped as well.

Complete, and rather large, car body/frame assemblies can be dipped as an assembly.

Redi-Strip

The nice thing about this process is the way it gets at all the surfaces...

...areas normally hidden from view, and any other means of stripping paint and rust, are stripped of all old paint, coatings and rust.

Unlike an acid dip, the two-step paint and rust removal process used by Redi-Strip removes paint and rust, and only paint and rust. There is no change to the thickness of the parts. If the fender comes out of the tank looking like someone shot it with a 12 gauge shotgun, it's because the rust was that bad. It's not because the process removed good steel.

FLASH RUST

When the parts come out of the de-rusting tank, they are dipped in a tank of rust inhibitor. The inhibitor will prevent flash rust, but this coating is water-soluble, so you don't want the parts to sit around for months protected by only this light coating. If it's going to be some time before the parts see primer, Redi-Strip can dip everything in a phosphate tank, and you can apply primer right over that

The plant we worked with is located in Milwaukee, but Redi-Strip is a franchised brand, and while there may not be one in your backyard, there are facilities scattered throughout the country. So just click on your browser and find the plant closest to you. Though it's not cheap, this process stands alone as an ideal way to remove paint and rust.

Q&A: John at Redi-Strip

John: How long have you been here at Redi-Strip?

I started here in college, that was 35 years ago. Now I own the facility.

How big an item or car body can you handle?

We can strip items up to 20 feet long, and handle weight up to 10 tons.

How long does it take to strip a complete body?

It depends on the body, the thickness of the paint and the amount of rust. We leave it in the strip tank for 24 hours, then inspect it, then it may have to go back in for another 24 hours. That's just the paint stripping part of the process. We still have to dip the part or parts in the de-rust tank.

What do people do wrong when they bring in a body or a collection of parts?

They don't disassemble them far enough. The more they disassemble it, the better job I can do. I can't get the rust out if it's hidden behind another part or panel.

Can you describe the complete process start to finish?

First, we get the job in the door and we take digital pictures. That way we all know what it is and what condition the body or the parts are in. We price the job before the customer leaves and fill out a contract. Next it goes into a basket, and we inventory the parts.

The actual stripping starts as we drop the body into an alkaline strip tank that's heated to180 degrees. It stays in the tank for 24 hours. Then it is rinsed. If there is still paint on, we put it back in the tank for another 24 hours.

Next, we wash it off and put the body and any parts into the electrolytic de-rust tank. This tank uses electrolysis to separate the iron oxide - rust – from the good metal.

Normally we get 50% of the rust during the first de-rust session. Of course the parts aren't evenly rusted. So it may take awhile to completely remove all the rust. The beauty of the process is the fact that it only takes the rust, the iron oxide. We don't hurt the metal. Our process is better than an acid dip, because we remove rust without attacking the steel. There is no change in dimension and no hydrogen ebrittlement.

The final step is the rinse and a dip in a tank of water-soluble rust inhibitor.

How much of your work is old trucks and cars?

Well, 80% of our work is industrial, the rest is automotive and small items for individual customers.

Any downside to the process?

It does take a while, people always want to know how come it takes so long.

Here's another complete assembly and one of the huge dip tanks. There really isn't any other way to completely strip an assembly like this.

into a variety of nooks and crannies, something you can't do with a sander or grinder.

SANDING

Perhaps the oldest and most common form of paint removal is sanding. Sanding will take the paint off, though it's not nearly as good on rust as the various blasting methods. If sanding has a downside, it can be summed up in one word – time. Sanding a fender or a whole vehicle to bare metal takes an enormous amount of time. If you try to speed up the process you run into problems similar to those encountered with sand blasting, too much heat. The big grinders, equipped with a coarse pad, will take off paint and filler in a hurry, as well as a fair amount of metal. What's left behind is often over-heated stressed metal that will be hard to work.

Sanding then should be done with an indirect or orbital sander and sandpaper that isn't too aggressive. In a body shop these sanders are simply referred to by two letters: DA. DA stands for double action, meaning the sanding pad isn't connected directly to the shaft or armature of the sander. Instead the motor drives a drum and the drum in turn drives the sanding or grinding pad. The net result is a sanding pad

Big grinder/sanders, like this seven inch air powered model...

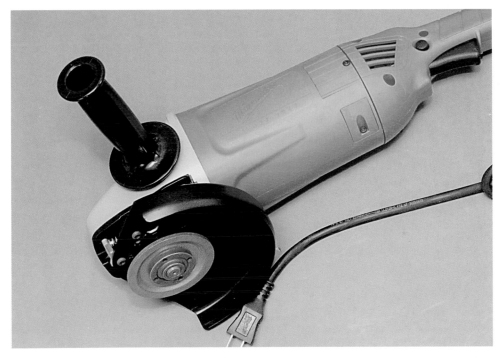

...and this nine inch electric, are better left to true grinding operations. These very powerful tools can score the metal and/or create enough heat to warp a panel.

that vibrates as much as it rotates so there are no swirl marks or gouges, and minimal heat build up. Many of these are available with a foam base for the sand paper which makes the action of the sand paper even less aggressive and helps the pad flex to match the contour of the metal being sanded.

All of this take time, however, which brings us back to the one reason most painters don't use sanding alone to remove a lot of paint, it simply takes too much time.

Unlike a conventional sander, a DA can sand a surface and take off paint without the typical gouging and swirl patterns...

CHEMICAL STRIP

The other obvious option open to anyone who wants to take off all the paint is a chemical strip. The word messy might best describe this option. The strippers are available from a variety of sources and include toxic and non-toxic examples. Generally the material is brushed on and left for a specific period of time to do its work. Then the stripper and paint-paste is scrapped off with a putty knife.

Suggestions include using a non-toxic biodegradable product as a way to protect your health, giving the product time to perform its chemical magic, and using plastic putty knives to avoid putting gouges in the metal.

After stripping off the paint, there will be small creases and areas that were missed by the chemical that

...the key is in this hub, which separates the disc from the motor. The net result is a sanding disc that vibrates as much as it rotates. With this model the hub can be locked so the DA becomes a conventional sander. Mississippi Welders Supply Co.

must still be dealt with. You can either sand the paint out of these small areas, or use coarse steel wool and another application of the stripper to get the last of the paint out of the creases and corners. The surface must be neutralized after the chemical is rubbed off and thoroughly flushed with water. And the smooth surface that's left behind will probably need to be scuffed with something like an 80 grit pad on a DA to provide the first coat of primer a surface it can easily adhere to.

THE CHEMICAL DIP

If stripping an old truck or tractor with liquid stripper is messy and the material doesn't get into the creases, why not dip the whole fender, or body, into a vat of liquid paint remover? The reason very few painters opt for this option is primarily because there aren't very many dip-strip operations in this country. Which means you will likely have to ship the body or parts by truck or take them there yourself. For help in deciding if this is the answer for your old tractor or truck, we've assembled a side-bar on dip-stripping in this chapter. We've also listed a few dip-strip operations in the Sources section, and ads can be found in Hemmings News.

It's too bad this process is somewhat difficult to utilize because in many ways it's the best option of all. It eliminates everything but the metal, including the body filler and any rust. What you get back is a bare steel fender, or complete body ready for any necessary panel repairs, coated only with some kind of light rust inhibiting solution. If you're lucky enough to have one of these facilities close to where you live, stop by and get a ten minute tour, this is an intriguing solution.

WHICH ONE

The method you use will depend on the project, as well as your budget for time and money. If it's an old tractor you just want to dress up and get running, then sanding off some of the paint with a DA might be the best alternative. If money's no object, or you want this old Oliver or Dodge to be better than new, you're going to want to strip off all or nearly all the old paint and any filler, and start over.

Remember, at the very least, you have to get down to something with enough integrity to act as the foundation for all the new paint to follow. To use the old barn analogy again, there is no point in repairing a house or barn that sits on a bad foundation.

Stick-on discs in all the common grits are available for a DA, which makes it really easy to just rip one off, stick on another and get back to work.

Chapter Five

The First Coats

Filler, Primer & Sealer

We've all head the term "primer", the paint that goes on first before the real paint goes on. Like anything else, when you really look at primer, it turns out there are at least four different sub-categories of paint that go on, "before the real paint does."

PRIMER

A pure primer is meant to adhere tenaciously to the material it's sprayed over. Ideally, primer should provide good resistance to corro-

Primer comes in a whole gamut of flavors. This oil based product is meant to be used under some of the Valspar enamel products. It's a good idea to buy the primer, sealer and topcoat paint from the same manufacturer so you know the products will work together without any adverse chemical reactions.

sion and a good surface that the next coat of paint can stick to. True primers aren't generally sanded.

PRIMER-SURFACER

A primer-surfacer, sometimes called a high-build primer, is a primer with a high solids content. The solids mean this product can be used to fill small scratches and irregularities in a panel. When painters want a panel really flat, they often spray three (or more) coats of high-solids primer, allow it to cure, block sand the panel, apply another three coats of primer and go through the whole block sanding sequence again, usually with a finer grit of paper the second time. Part of the key to making good use of these materials is to allow them to dry – and shrink fully - before the sanding so the panel doesn't change dimension after the sanding. Note the sanding sequences in Chapter Eight.

EPOXY-PRIMER

An epoxy or two-part primer is a super durable primer material known for superior bonding, high strength and corrosion resistance. As with other two-part products the catalyst used in an epoxy primer allows the paint molecules to cross-link like a fence that flexes but never tears. Most of the major paint companies have epoxy products that can be used as the first coat of paint applied to bare metal (always read the label and data

continued, page 49

House of Kolor makes some very good primer and paint products, including this two-part sandable primer.

Another House of Kolor product, this sealer will prevent the topcoat paint from soaking down into the filler material. Can be tinted to make topcoating easy.

Mud-less Dent Repair

Flat black hides a lot of imperfections, so it's a little hard to see the dent on the driver's side of the hood.

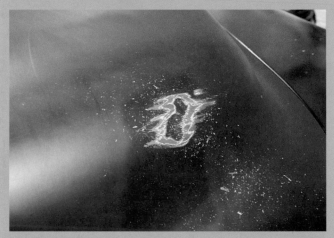

A vixen file, run over the dent, helps to make it really stand out.

Bruce starts with a body hammer and dolly.

The dent seen in the hood of the old Chevy is pretty typical of what you will find when restoring any old truck or tractor. It's a small enough dent that you might be tempted to just sand off some paint and apply a glob of your favorite filler. Bruce Bush has a better idea though, why not metal-finish the dent? Not only is it often faster then applying two coats of filler, with wait times and sanding between coats, metal finishing is simply the right thing to do.

"When someone tries to fix a dent like this without any filler," explains Bruce, "they tend to start by whacking the dent in the center to push it back out. But that's the wrong way to do it. What you should do is work from the outside of the dent to the center. You should do this in a spiral motion if you can."

THE WORK BEGINS

Bruce starts the job not with a hammer, but with a file. After a few licks with the file it's much easier to see the low spot. As explained above, the hammer work starts at the edge of the low spot. Bruce works from behind, hammering the edge of the low spot while holding a dolly on the outside. To assess the progress, he runs the file over the dent again. At this point there are a few high spots instead of one low spot. This calls for a little more hammer and dolly work, essentially the reverse of what was done in the first steps and with the use of a different dolly.

Most simple metal finishing is nothing more that the process described above. Raising low spots and knocking down high spots. The key is in not over stretching the metal. In knowing when to say when. Too much banging one way and then the other can work-harden the steel and make it brittle. The old trucks and tractors are pretty forgiving, however. The steel is pretty thick and very durable. You can push the metal around, file some of it off and still end up with a very acceptable repair that needs only a thin coat of filler, or just a few coats of high-built primer to be perfect.

Mud-less Dent Repair

While holding the dolly's flat side against the hood Bruce works the edges of the low spot from below.

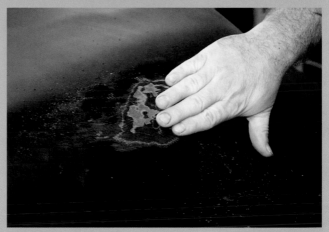

You have to train your hand to easily assess the damaged area.

Bruce gives the area a squirt of flat black and then goes over it again with the file...

Now Bruce uses a dolly with a contour that matches the curve of the hood...

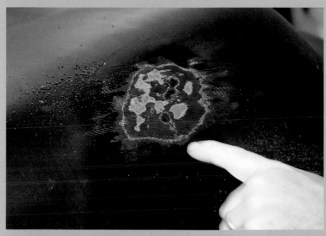

...here you can see how one low spot is now a bigger low spot with a series of high points.

The dolly is held in place underneath as Bruce works the high spots down with a series of soft blows.

Mud-less Dent Repair

A small sander is used to eliminate all the remaining paint...

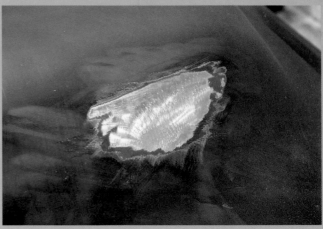

The area looks uniform and matches the contour of the surrounding metal.

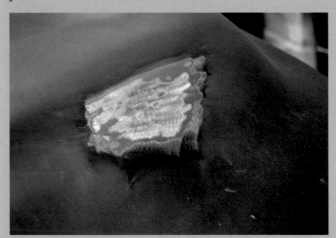

...which leaves the area with the uniform finish seen here.

The final finishing step is to sand the area with the DA and an 80 grit pad...

Bruce takes the top off any remaining high spots, and identifies remaining low spots, with a few passes of the vixen file.

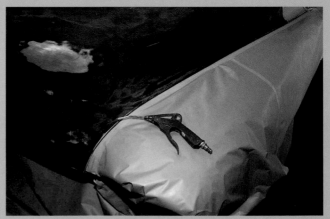

...which leaves the dent ready for primer, without the use of filler or even any spot putty.

sheets), and some can be sanded like a primer surfacer.

SEALER

A sealer is generally meant to be used after the primer and primer-surfacers, and before the final topcoats. A pure sealer is not meant to be sanded and has three jobs to do: act as a bond coat between the primer and topcoat; act as a barrier between the topcoat and the primer, preventing the topcoat from soaking into the primer which can affect the color and gloss of the topcoat; and make sure the vehicle is all one color before the topcoat is applied. Many modern sealers can be tinted, so the color is the same as, or similar to, the topcoat color. If the topcoat is being applied to a sealer of the same color the final paint will cover in fewer coats.

BARE METAL, WHAT COMES NEXT

Let's say you have the fender or hood down to bare metal, what comes next? If there are high and low spots in the panel that you can't eliminate with metal finishing, you're going to want to apply some filler. Many filler products are actually designed to be applied to a painted substrate, they want the filler applied to a really good primer like a two-part primer. Yet, many of the technicians working day to day in the body shops of the world apply their filler to bare metal. Many like to put some serious scratches in the panel so there's some "tooth" for the filler to adhere to. If you

Sealer is the paint you apply after the primer and before the topcoat or final color. The main goal is to ensure the topcoat paint doesn't sink into the primer and filler. Many of the new sealers can be tinted to match or nearly match the color of the topcoat paint.

When applying mud it helps to pull the mud all the way across the panel for a nice smooth application.

follow this practice just be sure you don't over-heat and stress the panel when you're in the process of creating the "tooth."

Manufacturers of most modern premium fillers explain that the material can be applied to primer and to scratches of only 80 grit rather than the 36 grit gouges that were necessary back in the day.

Before you decide to skip the hammer and dolly sequence and just throw on some filler, remember Bruce Bush's advice from Chapter Eight. It's actually faster to take as much of the dent out as possible before applying filler, instead of just putting the filler on as thick as needed to even out highs and lows.

MIX THE FILLER

One of the first successful two-part fillers went by the name Bondo, and that name became part of the vocabulary for anyone who did body and paint work. Today, the two-part fillers are manufactured by a host of companies, and each claims good adhesion and easy sanding.

A filler needs to be mixed according to the directions, not with more or less hardener than is called for to either speed up or slow down the hardening. Thorough mixing is critical, so there are no uncured areas in the panel that stay soft. Purists insist that the mixing be done carefully to avoid introducing air to the mix. You need to flatten it as you mix rather than just churning it like a cake mix. Air bubbles that show up later are just one more step that needs to be completed before you can do the final paint.

The companies that manufacture filler recommend that you mix the mud on a plastic pallet made for this job, and not on cardboard. The cardboard absorbs chemicals from the mixed material, and can also contaminate the filler.

What we call filler actually comes in a range of weights. Most current fillers are considered lightweight, or easy to sand. A fiberglass reinforced product like Duraglas is useful over a welded seam or when the filler needs to be extra thick. And spot putty is useful for little spots that were missed along the way.

Use of Two-Part Filler

A long time ago, men used semi-molten lead to fill creases or dents in fenders and doors, dents they couldn't remove through typical metal finishing methods. Besides being awkward to work with, lead is highly toxic. Then a new plastic product came to town promising faster set up and easier use. John Ballard is a man who understands filler. A man who sells a complete line of filler products for Evercoat, the manufacturer of Rage, one of the most well accepted and commonly used filler products in the body-shop industry. And when he isn't selling Rage he's often using the product. In concert with his father-in-law, John repairs and restores a variety of John Deere tractors.

John, tell me a little about yourself and how you came to work for Evercoat.

I've been in the auto body business for 25 years and sold lots of things along the way. I like being with Evercoat because everyone knows the brand, now I can spend the time telling them why the product will work for them.

We've all heard about filler, some of us still call it Bondo. Tell us a little about what it's actually made from and what makes a lightweight filler?

Our Rage filler is made up of three components: micro bubbles, which make for easier sanding, talc, and resin. The resin is what makes the bond, it's what makes a body filler great instead of just OK.

What about the relative weight of the body fillers?

Our Rage product is a light weight filler, There really aren't any heavy weight fillers anymore, though there are some fiberglass reinforced fillers which are good when you're trying to fill a deep void, or go over a welded seam or patch panel.

What makes Rage a premium filler and what do you get in the filler market when you spend more money?

Premium boils down to the quality of the resin. You can buy body filler at a discount store, but it's not the same. With ours, the adhesion is better, it will stick to bare metal or to sanded primer. With some fillers you get what they call 'mapping' after the job is finished, you can see where the repair work was done.

So you don't have to put this material on bare metal?

You can sand right down to the metal. You can also put it on top of two-part primer, or the factory primer if that's in good condition.

Tell us more about the surface that Rage can be applied to?

It used to be you had to go to bare metal with a 36 grit pad. Everyone said you needed the deep scratches so the filler would have something to hang onto. That's no longer the case. With a good filler like ours, all you need is an 80 grit scratch. On modern cars, the guys will use a 40 grit pad just to break through the clearcoat, then they switch to an 80 grit pad. You have to get all the paint off, but you don't have to get all the primer off. Next, they clean it. Too often people don't keep the area clean. Once it's clean, you can apply the mud. The first

All the good fillers are two part products, consisting of the filler itself and the hardener. Note the plastic pallet, no cardboard.

Use of Two-Part Filler

The hardener should be kneaded before being used. Always note the expiration date.

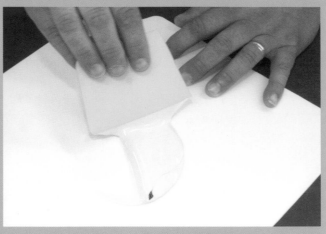

To mix the material, fold the filler over on itself, trying not to get the hardener on the squeegee.

With the Rage product they recommend a four inch puddle - as measured by a four inch squeegee.

Then mix the material further by pulling through the mix with downward pressure.

To get the correct ratio of filler to hardener, run one strip of hardener as shown across the four inch puddle.

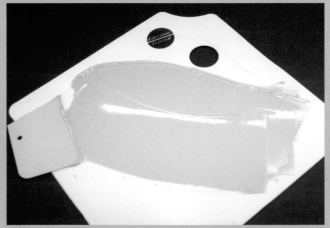

When it's fully mixed the material has a uniform color. A thin layer will extend the work time.

Use of Two-Part Filler

coat would be a tight wet coat. It's important to squeegee it on, that will minimize any pinholes. Be sure to get it into all the nooks and crannies. If you put it on too heavy the top coat crusts over and the filler underneath doesn't cure. Then sand that coat of filler with 80 grit, the same grit you used just before applying the filler.

After sanding with the 80 grit, follow with 180 grit. Depending on the condition of the panel, you can add another layer of filler, or apply a coat of a lighter product like a glaze. In our product line you can even mix the glaze into the Rage to create a hybrid product that's thicker than glaze but creamier than straight Rage.

How thick can a good filler be applied?

The filler shouldn't be any more than 1/4 inch thick when it's sanded. If you need more than that you need fiberglass reinforced body filler, which we already mentioned. It's good for a thicker application, or over a welded seam, because it seals better than the standard fillers.

Is it OK to begin shaping the filler before it's completely hard?

Yes. I like to drag a finder nail across it, if it dusts up on my nail then I figure it's time to start shaping. When you start sanding the dust will look almost moist, not powdery. Usually it's about eight minutes to get it to the point where it's cured enough to sand.

The video you have on the web site (evercoat.com/training) talks about the importance of mixing the filler and the hardener, is this a place people commonly make mistakes?

Yes, it's important that they add hardener in the right percentage, which is 2% by weight. A good way to control the amount of hardener is to start with a four-inch puddle of filler and run a line of hardener that goes all the way across. When you mix the two products, don't whip it, because you add air. The best method is to fold the filler over the hardener, so the hardener isn't on the applicator. After folding it repeatedly and mixing it with strong downward strokes, spread it over the pallet.

The pallet should be aluminum or glass or ceramic, not cardboard. Cardboard absorbs the resin from the filler and the filler picks up fibers.

Be sure to knead the hardener first, and if it comes out of the tube clear it's no good. Always note the date code on the tube of hardener. It has a one-year shelf life.

What are the other mistakes people make that compromise the performance of a good filler?

The worst problem, they add more or less hardener to get more or less work time. Second, they use a hardener from another paint company. Third, they put the filler on too thick. Fourth, they leave 40 grit scratches at the edge of the repair area, and the cleaning agents they use get trapped in those deep scratches and that causes sand scratch swelling later. You have to feather out the edges of the repair area so you don't have any of those deep scratches.

John Ballard is comfortable selling, or using, the latest in filler products.

Chapter Six

John Deere Green

Block Sanding and Single-Stage Paint

Painting a tractor is a lot like painting anything else, the job requires a certain amount of mechanical aptitude combined with patience and an eye for detail. Greg Anderson from Princeton, Minnesota is the man seen here painting the John Deere grille. A man who does everything from tractor restoration to typical crash repair, Greg explains that, "people think a part like this is easy to paint, but I'll have 35 or 40 hours in this grill by the time I'm through. Of course it was so beat up we had to cut some of the ribs loose, straighten them out and then weld them back in place."

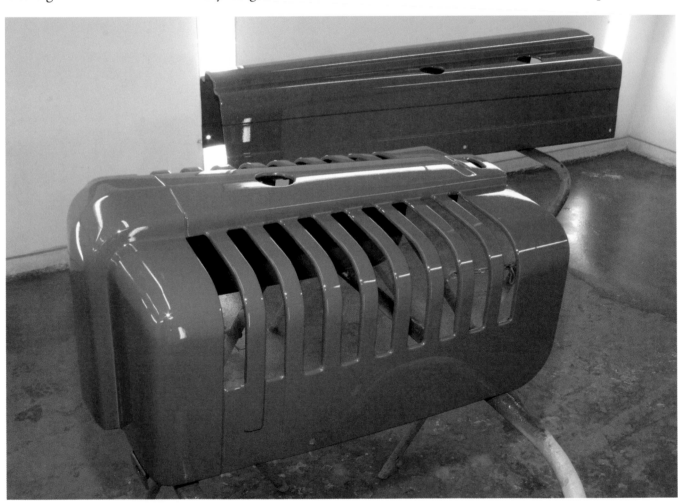

Whether you're painting John Deere green or Massey-Harris red, all the original colors are available in both enamel and urethane paint. This particular project was done using a single-stage urethane from Valspar.

The initial block sanding is done with a hard block, the primer is a two-part sandable product.

At this point, Greg has all the heavy bodywork finished and is near the end of the primer sequence.

Greg just keeps the sanding block skimming over the surface so the high spots are eliminated and the low spots are revealed.

The paper is 240 grit and Greg uses with plenty of water.

THE PROJECT

When we come on board Greg has all the heavy bodywork finished and is near the end of the primer and sanding sequence. The block sanding is being done with 240 grit paper on a hard block, the primer is a two-part sandable product. Greg just keeps the sanding block skimming over the surface so the high spots are eliminated and the low spots are revealed. Greg reminds painters that it's important to sand from more than one direction, "so you don't leave tracks in the primer." Another good trick is to use primer of different colors which makes it easy to see where the high and low spots are after sanding. As Greg explains, "each step of the sanding process should eliminate the sanding marks left by the preceding step."

From 240 grit on a hard block, Greg moves to 240 grit paper on a soft sanding pad. This combination is used to get at the sides of the ribs and

Greg reminds painters that it's important to sand from more than one direction "so you don't leave tracks in the primer."

Greg moves to 240 grit on a soft sanding pad.

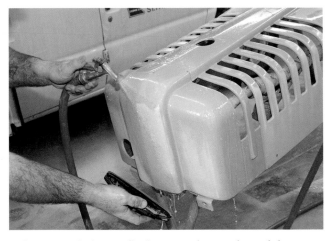

The water helps to flush away the sanding debris and keeps the paper from plugging up.

This combination is used to get at the nooks and crannies...

You have to be careful with corners, it's easy to sand through the primer to the paint below.

...and sides of the ribs missed by the hard block.

Part way through the block sanding sequence the grille is looking pretty good, note that Greg retained the subtle crease in the main, center rib.

any little nooks and crannies missed by the hard block. Next comes three more coats of primer. During the primer application, Greg explains the importance of the correct technique for a part like this, "What people forget, especially when they are starting out, is that the paint won't wrap around corners, you have to change the angle of the gun all the time especially with something like this grille."

After the primer cures Greg starts another block sanding sequence with 400 grit, used wet like the earlier block sanding. Before moving on to the next stage in the sequence, Greg wipes the parts down with wax and grease remover.

SEALER

The importance of using sealer can't be overstated. The main goal of the sealer coat is to ensure the green topcoat won't soak down into the primer.

continued, page 61

Greg is careful to sand all the surfaces...

...even those between each rib. "Block sanding is the most important part of the prep process, key part of the sequence."

Greg wipes the parts dry before he applies the next coats of primer.

The next coats of primer go on using a gravity-feed HVLP gun.

Again, Greg is careful to apply the paint from various angles to as to get the primer on all the surfaces.

In this light, with the wet paint, you get some idea how nice and flat the panels are.

The primer needs to cure according to the manufacturer's directions before the next round of block sanding (not shown) can begin.

Before applying sealer it's important to blow off the parts and wipe them down with a tack rag.

The sealer is a single-stage product. Greg applies it...

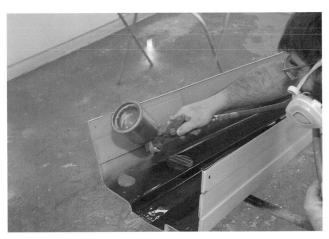

The idea is to always...

...with nice straight passes...

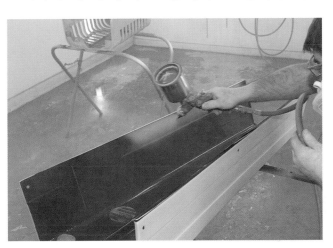

...keep the spray gun perpendicular to the object being painted...

...each one overlapping the last by 50%.

...and to apply the paint to objects like the grille from numerous angles so all the surfaces are covered by paint.

The cups provided by the manufacturer make it easy to get all the materials mixed in the right amounts.

This single stage paint uses a hardener, which means it should be sprayed and handled with care.

The throw away liners like this are available for most good spray guns and make clean up much easier.

Just fill the liner and get ready to attach the cup to the gun.

The well-worn gun in this case is a SATA HVLP with a gravity-feed cup.

This particular paint is a single-stage product.

The second goal for the sealer is to make the part one color. Even better than making the sheet metal one color, is to make that color something close to the color of the topcoat - which makes it easy to cover in a minimum number of coats. Greg uses a dark sealer, which will make it easy to get good coverage with another dark color, John Deere green.

To make the process as efficient as possible, Greg starts by sealing the inside of the grille, then follows up with two coats of the John Deere Green. Each sealer product states the ideal time for topcoating, anyone who waits too long and misses the "window" will have to sand the sealer before coming back in to apply the topcoat. As mentioned earlier, if the topcoat is applied within the recommended window the paint will bond chemically with the sealer underneath. If you wait too long however, to apply the topcoat you loose the opportunity for the chemical bond. In this case, the sealer should be sanded so there will be a mechanical bond in place of the chemical bond.

ON TO THE GREEN

The final paint is a single-stage Valspar product, Omega 2K, Low VOC Polyurethane. Unlike the two-stage paints seen farther along in this project, the Omega is the color and it dries with a gloss finish, no clearcoat needed. Greg explains that in the case of the single-stage paint, "it's a

The topcoat is mixed with reducer, chosen to match the temperature of the shop, and activator.

Once the sealer has dried (each product is different) Greg puts the first coat of green on the inside.

Again, each pass is straight and true, made without interruption. The next pass overlaps the first by 50%.

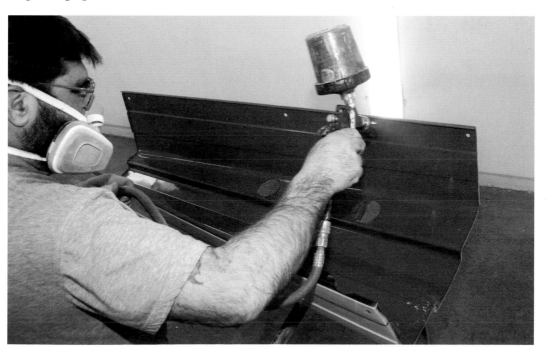

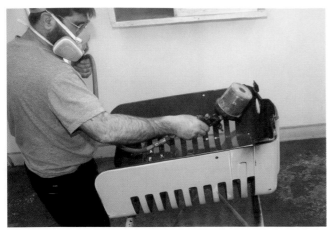

Working within the sealer's window of time, Greg applies the John Deere green to the inside of the grille.

Again, Greg applies the paint from different angles to ensure all the grill's irregular surfaces are covered.

good idea to apply the first coat a little light to avoid runs, then follow that up with a heavier coat." When the inside of the grille is dry enough Greg flips the grille over and repeats the process on the outside. The only difference between the inside and outside of the grille is the extra coat Greg applies to the outside surfaces.

"Because this is a new paint to me," explains Greg, "I'm going to put on a light coat just to get the feel for the paint, then come back and do a second coat. In fact, if you're using a product like this for the first time it's a good idea to take an old fender or panel and prep it like you do the regular parts and then practice painting on that. Without some practice, the first-time painter is going to have runs."

Greg warns that, "with a single-stage paint you can put the coats on too fast. The paint has to get pretty dry before you add another coat. It should not string up on your finger when you touch it, but your finger should leave an impression. If it does string up on your finger just walk away until it does. How quick it dries is affected by the shop temperature and the amount of air movement."

Working in this careful fashion and with the required wait time between coats, Greg applies a total of three coats of John Deere Green to the hood and grille.

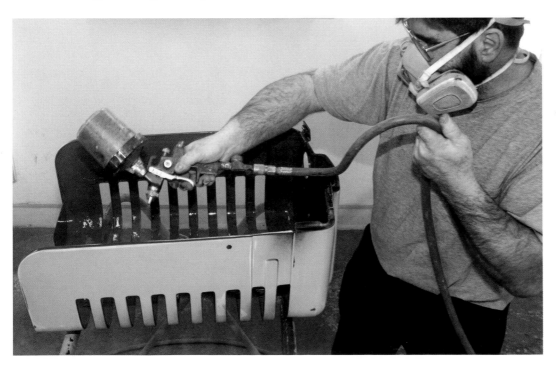

Unlike the outside of the panels, the inside of the parts get one coat of finish paint.

With the underside of the panels painted, Greg begins applying sealer to the outside of the hood. Note how neat and precise each pass is.

...applied to all the surfaces.

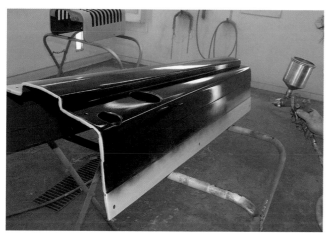

Greg uses the body lines as natural guides and an easy way to lay out nice straight lines with 50% overlap between passes.

By the time he's finished with the sealer on the grille, enough time has passed that Greg can begin to apply the John Deere green to the hood.

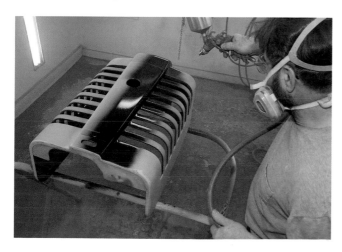

Back to the grille, which gets one coat of sealer...

Again, the body lines make guides that make it easier to lay out nice straight passes.

The left side of the hood gets the same treatment.

Though it's sometimes difficult, it's likewise very important to keep the gun perpendicular to the surface at all times.

Here you can see the last pass of the first coat of green.

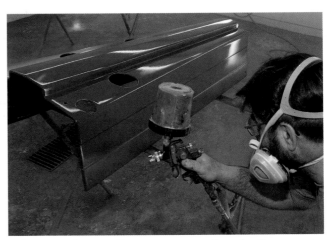

The second coat of green goes on after the first coat is still soft, but does not string up on a finger. Each pass is made from edge to edge, moving the gun at a consistent speed.

Just as he did when applying the primer and the sealer, Greg applies the topcoats to the grille from a variety of angles.

Here Greg applies the second coat of green to the grille.

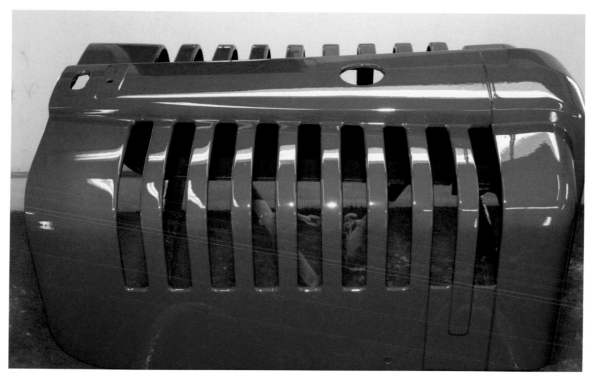

Here's the grille, hard to believe it was a piece of junk when Greg started.

When the paint is wet and fresh, you can really see any little flaw in the panels. This is when all that careful block sanding pays big dividends.

Chapter Seven

Tractor Painting

The Massey gets Painted Factory Red

The subject of our Tractor-Painting chapter is a 1952 Massey-Harris Pony belonging to Greg Anderson. Greg is a certified Massey enthusiast. In fact, Greg's passion for Massey tractors might be genetic, as his grandfather, and later his Father Gary, ran the Massey-Harris dealership in Greg's hometown of Princeton, Minnesota.

The renovation starts as Greg pulls the old girl out of the barn and onto a trailer. Eventually the little Massey ends up at Greg's shop, Anderson Tire, located along the highway just south of Princeton.

Repainting an old tractor isn't rocket science, but it is a lot of work. Take a look at the next page to see what this nice old Massey looked like "before." To succeed you need good products and a good plan. Remember to get something done every week so the project doesn't stall.

DISASSEMBLY AND ASSESSMENT

"The first thing to do," explains Greg, "before taking it apart, is an assessment. Figure out what you have, what is missing, and which parts you are going to have to order. Order the parts now so they are on hand when you're ready for the assembly. Next, record the sizes of the tires and get the serial number off the engine and the frame."

In this case we are missing things like the shifter boot, tie-rod boots, toolbox and side tins. In addition, Greg decides to order the standard maintenance items like a cap and rotor, ignition wires, a wiring harness, new amp and oil-pressure gauges, and a belt. Some of these components, like the gauges and wiring harness, can be "ordered" from his own small company (Anderson Implement) which manufactures hard-to-find Massey parts like gauges and wiring harnesses.

Greg grabs a collection of cardboard boxes and plastic bags so all the parts and bolts can be kept in appropriate groups. This provides another opportunity to inventory the parts, and also promises to make the assembly much easier.

Anderson Tire is more than a tire store. In addition to mechanical work, the crew does a wide range of body and paint work. The Pony becomes one more project in an already crowded work area.

SANDBLASTING

The sheet metal comes off first, then the hood, fenders, and the optional headlights. "Be sure to take plenty of pictures of everything before you rip it all apart," advises Greg. "The pictures will help you get the right bolts in the right holes and the wires routed the right way. They really help."

"For the sandblasting we are using regular sand," explains Greg. "There's a black sand that's more aggressive, but it's hard to find. Remember, the sandblasting creates heat, which can warp the sheet metal. You need an experienced operator so the sand hits the sheet metal at an angle, a glancing blow. You never want to hit it straight."

continued, page 75

This is where most of these tractor projects start - in a barn or an old shed where the tractor has been stored.
Captions by Greg Anderson.

Here we are pulling the tractor out of the barn with Duke the dog supervising.

Start disassembling slowly and take a lot of time to assess damage and problems.

1. Take a lot of pictures before you start and during the disassembly.

2. In our case the hood would be fixed, but the grill was pretty far gone.

3. Once you have the radiator out, be sure to have it pressure tested and combed so it's ready to go back in when you start the reassembly.

4. Lay out all of the parts and figure out what to fix or replace.

5. Sandblasting - you will come to love it.

6. No dirt or blasting sand in the gas tank - be careful.

Filling the pressurized blasting pot. Sandblasters like this are available from any good tool warehouse.

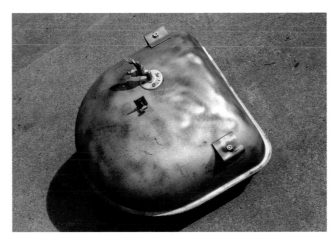

This gas tank has been blasted and is ready for sanding with 80 or 180 grit, then a coat of primer.

More sandblasting. I told you, you will get to love it.

Parts that are not going to receive bodywork or filler are sealed with primer right after sandblasting to avoid any flash rusting.

On sheet metal, hold your blasting tip farther away from the part so you don't warp the metal.

These chassis parts get their first coat of primer.

Decals don't sandblast off. Peel them off first.

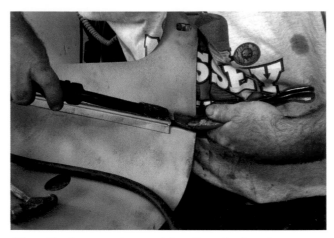

Here I'm hammering and bending the hood into shape.

Hold your blaster at an angle to the light sheet metal to avoid warpage.

50 years of abuse takes a lot of time to fix.

This hood is ready for 80 or 180 grit sanding. Then, wash with an acid-based cleaner.

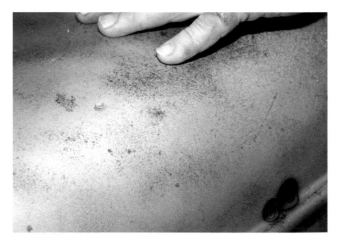

Note the rust embedded into pits in the metal. Acid-wash will neutralize this before sealing.

PRIMING, SEALING AND HOOD REPAIR

The sandblasting leaves the metal ready for paint or filler, and the parts are divided into two groups. Items like the gas tank are taken to the paint booth where they get a first coat of primer. Items that need bodywork, such as the hood, stay in the main work area where Greg mixes the first batch of filler. There are a number of small dents in the hood. Greg takes most of these out with a hammer and dolly, working slowly across the surface, checking the surface often with the palm of his hand. When done, he makes the comment, "You know these hoods weren't any better than this when they were new, they had some ripples and unevenness in the metal. We could just go ahead and paint it, but I'm going to skim the whole thing with filler. When we're done the sheet metal will probably be better than new."

Next, Greg goes over the whole thing with a DA equipped with an 80 grit pad, just to take off some of the roughness that's left from the sandblasting. The next step is a thorough wipe-down with wax and grease remover.

THE MUD

Greg mixes up enough filler to go over about half the hood. He mixes it very thoroughly, explaining, "if you don't get it mixed well you end up with soft spots in the middle after everything else has cured." The first coat is uniform and thin as shown. "Once I start to sand this we will probably find a few low spots that need a second coat. You can start to work the mud before it's fully set, but if you work it too soon and it starts to pull away you have to strip off all the mud from that area and start over. You can save a tremendous amount of time by working it before it's totally cured, but you have to be really careful."

Sanding the first coat of filler is done with an air file equipped with 36 grit paper. Note how the high and low spots are readily apparent after one or two passes with the power stick. He moves along the seam from front to back, and then moves from side to side.

continued, page 74

Here I'm hammering out the dents with a body hammer while I hold a dolly up against the back side...

...it's nice to be able to get at both sides of the panel, sometimes you need to use the sharp end of the hammer.

With the DA (double-action sander) I'm using 80 or 180 grit paper to smooth out the roughness left from sandblasting.

71

80 grit sandpaper on a dual-action (DA) sander.

Here I begin to apply a skin coat to the entire hood after I have all the dents worked out.

Before applying filler, I use wax and grease remover on all the metal parts.

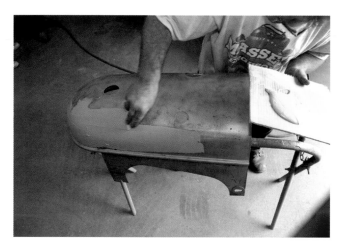

Apply a nice even thin coat...

Mix only as much filler as you can apply before it gets hard.

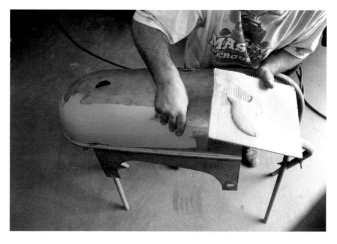

...with careful strokes of the squeegee.

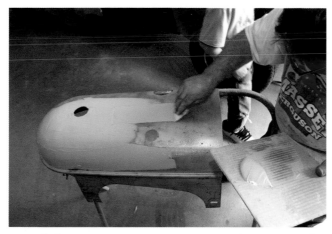

Avoid the temptation to put on more than you really need.

This tool is called an air file - a very valuable time saver.

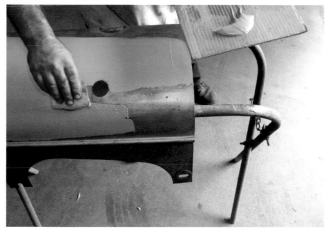

The idea is to apply a thin coat of filler over the entire hood.

I use 36 grit on the air file to level off high spots in the filler.

Make your application as smooth as possible. This will save you a lot of time when you start sanding.

Keep working the air file in all directions and float it over all the surfaces.

Sometimes it is harder to hold the panel in place than actually sand it.

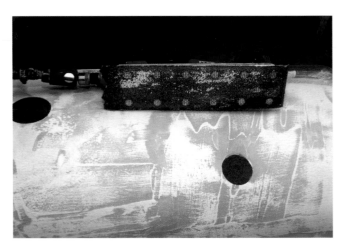

Here I have 36 grit on the air file. This is a short air file, they also make a longer one for longer panels.

The more you shave down the high spots the more the low spots will disappear.

A Second Application of Filler

Most panel repair requires at least two applications of filler and this hood is no different. Greg mixes a little more filler and applies it carefully to the low spots, smoothing the material as much as he can with the plastic applicator. "The neater you can put on the mud the less work you have later to sand it smooth. You should watch the guys who tape sheet rock, they're amazing, they never put on any more than they really need." Greg lets the second applications cure until it starts to set up and then sands again with more 36 grit on the air-file. When the hood is starting to look pretty good, he switches to 80 grit paper on a sanding pad.

"What we are doing is filling small voids left from the first coat, there may be small holes yet, we will fill those with finishing putty, but basically we go right into primer from here. The pad I'm using is a hard pad, not flexible,. A flexible pad used at this stage would not get it as flat as you want. With this hood, it's like trying to make an egg smooth, the sides and the top I want straight and smooth and the nose I want round."

When he has the hood looking pretty good, Greg uses a little catalyzed spot putty to fill the small low spots and voids and to fill any pin holes. This material sets up fast, ten minutes at the most. Greg sands the spot putty with the same grit that was used on the surrounding mud, 80 grit in this case.

Primer and Sandable Primer

Once the entire hood is sanded smooth and finished with 80 grit paper, Greg applies the first coat of the Valspar DTM product, mixed as a primer and tinted red. Note that even when he is applying the primer Greg uses a careful pattern of carefully spaced horizontal passes.

Even though the DTM can be used as a sandable primer, Greg wants to do more sanding to get the panels nice and flat. So after applying the DTM he applies multiple coats of two-part sandable primer. "I wait 10 minutes," explains Greg, "then put on another fairly heavy coat, then wait over night so it's had time to cure." The sanding

continued, page 79

Here I'm working the air file from the seam on the side to the top and then back down again.

At this point it looks like a pinto pony.

These low spots will need to be filled, it's hard to get it perfectly smooth with only one application of filler.

Then, back to the air file.

With the second application of filler, just fill the low spots not the whole hood.

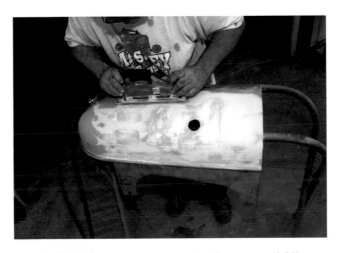

Level all of the spots down to the first coat of filler.

More air filing...

Then, it is time to use a hard sanding block with 80 grit to finish the filler.

...to eliminate the high spots in the filler and create a smooth, flat surface.

Here I'm sanding the long way on the hood with the hand sanding block and 80 grit paper.

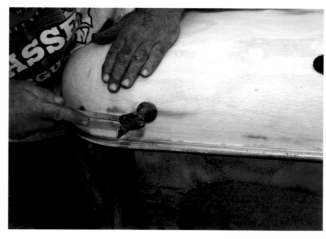

When we get close to having our filler finished we find a high spot of metal - so a little light tapping with the body hammer is called for.

Even after two coats of filler and plenty of sanding, a few small low spots remain.

These remaining low spots are filled with spot putty.

I do a little more block sanding with 80 grit paper...

As I look over the hood I find a few more small imperfections on the lower left corner.

...before beginning application of the DTM tinted primer.

Hand sand the putty with 80 grit on a hard block, the same grit I used on the last sanding sequence.

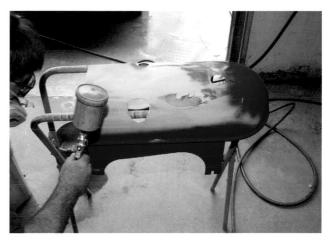

I put on a heavy coat and let it dry at least one hour.

Cover everything with primer.

After the red primer has dried I apply sandable primer.

Even though this is just a primer coat I apply the paint carefully with straight even passes.

I put on one heavy coat and wait approximately 10 to 15 minutes...

I like to let the primer dry at least one hour.

...before applying another heavy coat of sandable primer.

sequence, seen nearby, starts with 240 grit on a DA (320 could also be used) followed by 400 grit on a flexible pad, used with plenty of water.

THE GAS TANK AGAIN

The tank is actually part of the hood, so it needs to be finished to the same level of perfection as the hood. As was seen a few pages back, Greg started with sandblasting, then painted the tank with primer followed by the tinted primer. The next application of paint is multiple coats of sandable primer. After the first coat of sandable primer Greg block sands the top of the tank with 240 grit wet. Next comes more sandable primer and then additional sanding with a 240 grit pad on the DA (note the nearby photos). The work with a DA is followed with additional block sanding, done with 400 grit wet. The nice thing about having a layer of red primer under the sandable primer is the fact that any high spots show up red when the two-part primer is sanded off.

THE HOOD AND GRILLE GO RED

Greg follows a very specific sequence for the application of final paint on the hood and grille. "I paint the back side first (not shown), then we can mask the back off and do the top and sides. You can't do them both at once, it's just too hard to be flipping them over and trying not to mess up the paint during the process."

The grill is painted with some kind of primer from the factory, "the paint seems really nice so I sanded it and then will go from there." explains Greg. "I sanded the paint with 400 grit wet and then we're ready for paint, the sealer will have no trouble filling those 400 grit scratches. First I apply two coats of the tinted sealer (DTM mixes as a sealer) and then two coats of the finish red."

"Once the backside is painted you have to mask it off with tape, otherwise when you paint the front, the overspray comes through and leaves overspray on the back side."

LITTLE RED TRACTOR HOOD

With the back of the grille and the hood masked off, Greg wipes the top surfaces with wax and grease remover, then a tack rag. The sealer is applied in two coats, using nice straight passes,

continued, page 82

After the sandable primer is fully cured I start working over the hood with 240 grit on a small DA...

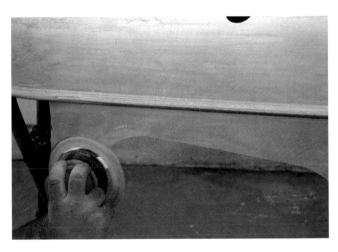

...the sides get the same treatment.

As does the top of the gas tank. Like we said earlier, this will be finished to the same level as the hood.

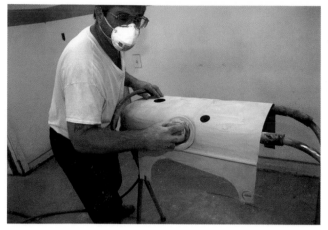

When you're using the DA..

The 400 grit paper is wrapped onto a soft sanding block.

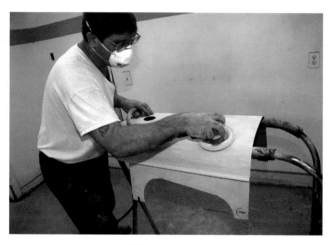

...be very careful to follow the contours.

The soft pad makes it easier to follow contours as I do the final wet sanding.

Now I do the final sanding using 400 wet.

Be sure to get under and around all of the edges and body lines.

I'm using the same 400 wet on the grille. I am going to paint right over this factory primer.

A stand like this is very handy. Before applying sealer it's important to wipe the hood off with wax and grease remover.

The inside of all the panels is painted first, then masked off...

Use wax and grease remover on all the parts that need to be painted.

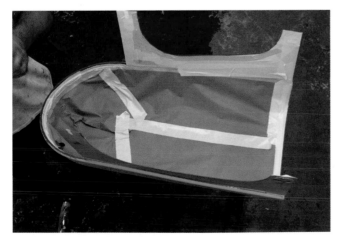

...the inside of the hood gets the same treatment.

Now I can put DTM tinted red and mixed as a sealer on the grille, hood and gas tank.

This is the first coat of sealer being applied to the grille...

...and the hood.

Again, be sure to get under and around all of the edges and body lines.

each one overlapping the other by 50%. With a complex shape like the grille, he paints from three different angles so he is sure to get paint on all the surfaces.

OOPS

After applying two coats of sealer, Greg notices a dent on the hood that was missed. This is easy to do, as small dents really show up in fresh, wet, shiny paint. And though the temptation might be to just "let it go," Greg decides that we've come too far to compromise the job at this late date.

Fixing the dent isn't that difficult. Greg starts by baking the paint to speed the cure. Next, he uses spot putty in the low area. Unlike filler, the putty can be applied over paint. Greg simply applies it neatly with a rubber squeegee. This is a fine grade of filler so it sands really nice. Even without heat it will cure in fifteen minutes.

Greg shaves the high spots with 80 grit on a block, follows that with 180 and finishes with a little 220. After sanding, however, it's obvious that we need another coat of glaze. So Greg puts on one more thin coat and goes through the sanding sequence again. This time though he finishes with a 320 grit pad on a DA to feather out the edges.

FINAL COATS

Greg puts a coat of tinted sealer on the recently repaired area, and then gets ready to apply the final paint to the hood and gas tank. The sealer is such a close match to the final paint color that it's hard to tell one from the other. Using the careful, straight passes again, Greg applies two coats of the finish paint - the specially mixed Massey red from Valspar. Each coat must flash before being topcoated with another, a process that takes about fifteen minutes.

Before the clear can be applied Greg wipes the parts off with a tack rag. Now he finishes the job with two coats of clear. As with the finish paint and the sealer, he allows each coat to flash off before applying the next.

The end result is a bright red Massey-Harris, looking way better than it ever did when it was new.

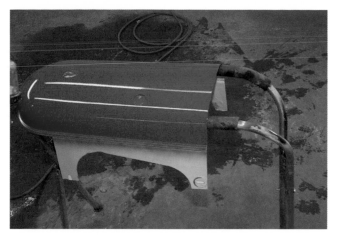

Once we have our red sealer on we found an 'oops.'

I block sand the area, starting with 80 grit and then progressing to 220.

The spot putty is two-part polyester based product. It dries fast and can be applied over paint on small areas.

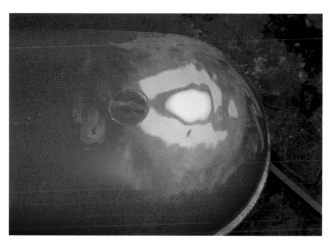

After block sanding it's obvious we need another coat of poly filler to flow out the repair.

A light coat of poly filling over dried sealer is okay.

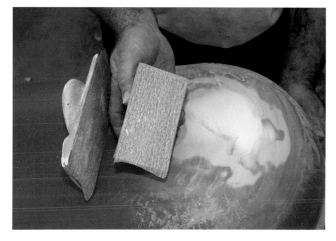

Once the second coat cures I start with 180 grit on a block.

Next I do some light sanding with a DA equipped with 320 grit paper.

I let the sealer dry and then use the tack rag to dust off the hood.

Tack rag all the dust off the hood...

Though the sealer flashes in 15 minutes, the directions recommend you wait at least 30 minutes, up to a max of one hour, before applying the color.

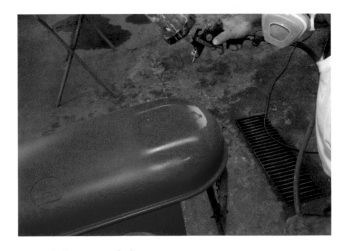

...and then reseal the area.

Shooting the first coat of color on the hood. The red sealer makes it easy to get good coverage.

The sealer is a such a close match to this finish paint that you have to be careful to monitor the progress.

Here's the grille...

Here I'm finishing up the application of the first coat of color.

...the gas tank...

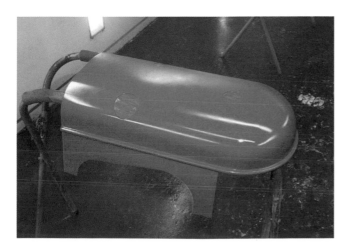

This is the hood after the first coat of color has flashed and I've applied the second coat.

...and the hood after the final coat of clear.

Q&A Greg Anderson

How long have you been doing body and paint work? And how did you get involved with tractors?

I've been doing bodywork for 27 years. Both my father and my grandfather were Massey-Harris dealers. And of course I was born and raised on the farm. I think though that it was my grandfather, Gil Anderson, who got me working on the tractors. He was the one who got me hooked. He opened the dealership in 1942, and sold new tractors until the mid 1950s. Eventually my Father, Gary, became involved, and then it was Anderson and Son. They sold used equipment right up into the 1980s.

When we were in the shop, you talked about looking over the vehicle before the work starts. Can you talk more about this and about determining how far you're going to go with the vehicle?

Once you decide to do the tractor, you have to do a walk around, take notes. What do you need? Do you need wiring harness tranny work? It's like doing an estimate for a car. We know 95% ahead of time, there will be some surprises, but not very many. People need to decide if they do have the where with all to do a project of that magnitude. They have to decide up front if they can do it or not. No point in getting it half done and then running out of money or time. Can I afford it, do I have time? It's a labor of love, like a street rod.

When it comes to painting and bodywork, what separates old tractors and trucks from more modern vehicles?

You have to repair everything. No new parts. When it comes in you have to rebuild and, or, repair everything. When a new Ford pickup truck comes in, I call and order new parts from the dealership. With an old tractor, every piece has to be done by hand. You have to be pretty mechanically inclined to work on this stuff.

The metal is much heavier on these vehicles than it is on more modern vehicles. Does that make the bodywork more or less difficult?

The heavier the gauge the nicer it is to work with in terms of straightening. But some of the parts were made from lighter material. The fenders were made from lighter steel because they didn't have heavy presses. They couldn't do a complex shape in a heavy gauge steel panel. On the Pony, the hood is 16 gauge, but the side tins are 22 gauge. So you get a lot of torn bolt holes and vibration cracks in that lighter material.

How do you approach rust? Do you cut it out or neutralize it?

It depends on how bad the rust is. I like to sandblast the panel and then analyze it. If it's not rusted through I neutralize it with something, a light acid-base for example. But you have to blast it first.

If it's rusted through then of course you have to cut out the rust and weld in a new panel. The nice thing about a sandblaster, when you're done you know how much good metal you have. People say, 'I don't want to blast it because it will blast through,' but that is what you want. You want to learn how good the metal really is.

For a person working at home, do you recommend single or two-stage paint, and why?

I recommend a two-stage paint. Basecoat and clearcoat. The new base/clear paints are so user friendly, it's almost hard to tell people not to use them. With the old single stage you need to be a good painter, If you can paint acrylic enamel you can paint with anything. But I hear that some of the judges are taking points off for basecoat/clearcoat.

What are the most common mistakes made by first-time and non-professional painters?

They don't put on enough paint. Not enough sealer, not enough primer or sealer, they try to skimp and save money. There is a process to painting and you have to follow it, you can't cheat the process if you expect to create a quality job.

Q&A Greg Anderson

What is the sequence you like to follow once you have bare metal?

Apply an epoxy primer, followed by sandable primer. Then at least 2 coats of color and 3 coats of clear.

What's required for a spray gun and compressor?

You should have at least a five horse compressor. For a gun, a hundred dollars will buy a good-enough gun, you don't have to buy a real expensive spray gun.

The other big problem people in small shops have is condensation. You have to have a water trap on the line leading to your gun, without that you set yourself up for huge flaws. You get moisture in the paint, the moisture creates rust blisters later. And the water is hard on all the air equipment. Remember that if the air compressor runs too long it gets hot and then puts an oil mist into the air.

We bought a refrigerated system for the air system in the shop, it's a great buy, the process cools the air so the water condenses and is removed from the air. There's a filter as well to remove oils, and foreign particles. Then it heats it again, so you don't get condensation farther down the line.

You can buy a home-sized unit for $350.00. You really need one of these if you are going to sandblast, otherwise you end up blasting with damp sand. It plugs up the blaster and is a really big problem.

We bought ours from a paint supply store, I know Northern tools sells them. Anyone who sells air compressors probably sells these refrigeration systems.

How about a shop, what is required for a shop and paint booth?

For a shop, all you really need is a 24 by 24 foot garage. You could do a small tractor in a space like that easily.

You need an enclosed area for your booth. Some guys just hang curtains in one corner. You don't need a fancy booth, just a room you can close off and a fan to create some airflow.

Greg Anderson comes from a long line of Massey-Harris enthusiasts, including his father and grandfather.

THE CHASSIS

Disassemble, Paint & Assemble

Unlike the sheet metal, painting the chassis is more about getting everything clean than it is about removing dents and sanding the filler. Greg and his crew spent hours and hours scraping off the big stuff and then cleaning the rest with solvent and brushes. Some of the parts had to be disassembled for repair, and these sub-assemblies were then cleaned thoroughly before being bolted back onto the tractor. Greg did the final cleaning with thinner, after areas where he didn't want paint were all masked off.

Unlike a truck or car, which utilizes a separate frame, most tractors use what might be called a backbone. Things like the bell housing and transmission case are internal chassis parts. The key is to completely disassemble the chassis, repair worn out components and then clean and re-clean everything before painting begins.

THE PAINT

Rather than use a separate primer and sealer, Greg used the same tinted DTM sealer from Valspar that was used on the sheet metal. As already mentioned, this paint requires no sanding between coats and sets up very flat. Because it's being used as a sealer and not a sandable primer, Greg mixes the sealer to a 4-1-2 ratio.

This paint starts as a neutral gray, there are five toners that are used in various percentages to duplicate nearly any finish color. Greg used the Valspar chart to match the primer to the Massey red. Like most modern sealers, this one has a top-coat window. Valspar recommends waiting at least 30 minutes, and not more than 24 hours, before topcoating with the basecoats.

The idea is to let the paint dry long enough that most of the solvents have escaped, but not so long that the new coat of paint can't bond chemically with the earlier coat of paint. If you wait too long you have to scuff the paint before putting on another coat – to create mechanical adhesion that takes the place of the (lost) chemical adhesion.

THE FIRST APPLICATION

As Greg begins applying the first coat of sealer, he's careful to come at the parts from different angles so there are no nooks and crannies and low spots in the castings that don't get coated by paint. Greg allows the first coat of sealer to flash before applying coat number two. After two coats of primer-sealer, and a wait of nearly an hour, **The First Basecoat.**

Like the sheet metal, the chassis is being painted with the Valspar basecoat-clearcoat system. Again, he comes at the various chassis parts from different directions. The second coat of basecoat can be applied after all the gloss is gone from the first, (but not more than 24 hours).

The last coats are the clear, and these require that the painter use a fresh air hood because the paint is catalyzed with isocyanates.

Greg applies two coats of the clear, allowing the first coat to go dull before applying the second. The end result is much like the sheet metal, a chassis that's more colorful and finished to a much higher level than it was when new.

The frame has been blasted and cleaned, all new bushings and pins have been installed.

Here, I'm masking off parts and places where I don't want to paint - like the inside of the tranny.

Once it's all masked off, I use wax and grease remover and blow it all dry.

We tint the DTM sealer and reduce it just like we did for the sheet metal.

Use sealer on all of the parts. Use a heavy coat on the cast iron parts.

These parts have all been blasted, primer sanded and are now ready for tinted sealer.

You must get right down and dirty to make sure you get sealer everywhere.

You have to be sure to get paint on all the surfaces, which involves getting under the chassis to spray the bottom.

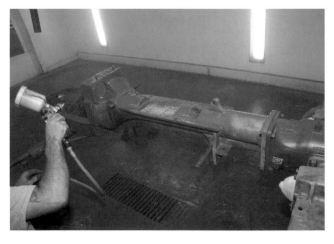

It takes patience to get underneath and around everything.

The sealer needs to dry for about an hour before you come back with the basecoat.

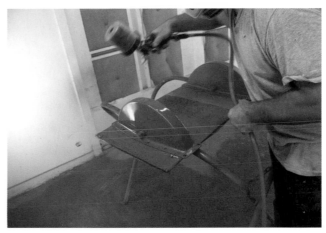

Here I'm applying the basecoat to some of the chassis parts...

After two coats of sealer the parts look finished, but there's still basecoat and clear to follow.

...and then to the chassis itself. Here again you will have to get down and dirty to get paint on all the surfaces.

Next comes the basecoat color, and the reducer that's best for the temperature in the shop.

Clear coat, reducer and catalyst, the last step.

Ready for clear.

Third coat applied and we are done with the chassis.

First coat will dry to the touch in about 15 minutes. "Dry" means the paint does not string-up when you touch it with your finger.

...except for a few big ugly components, like these wheels we painted with sandable primer so Casey could finish them with a 180 grit pad.

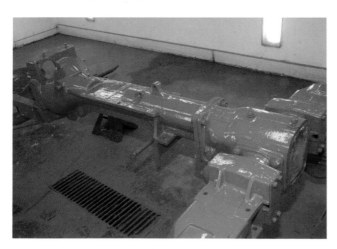

After the second coat of clear, we have one very red chassis.

Now comes the fun part - putting hundreds of parts all back together.

THE ENGINE
Disassemble, Paint & Assemble

Painting the engine is in some ways easier than the chassis, if for no other reason than because it's smaller, and it usually gets cleaned as part of the overhaul process. In the case of the little Massey four-banger, the engine came out of the tractor and went immediately to the shop of Gary Anderson, Greg's father. After disassembly, all the major components took a dip in the hot tank, followed by a thorough scrubbing with soap and water. Greg warns that you have be careful to clean the block again after it comes back from the machine shop, because it's usually covered with grinding particles from the machining and boring.

Rebuilt and painted in fresh Massey-Harris red. People are often intimidated to paint an engine, yet it's really no different than painting anything else, cleanliness and preparation are the two key components to a successful engine paint job.

Here's our motor back from being rebuilt.

The motor needs to be cleaned because it's very dirty from the rebuilder's shop.

It takes a lot of time and patience to clean the engine properly, but if it's not clean the paint won't stick.

Once Gary delivers the engine to Anderson Tire, Greg suspends it from the cherry picker and begins washing it down with brake cleaner and compressed air. The brake cleaner is nice as it leaves no residue behind. After applying the cleaner he uses a blow gun to blow any dirt down, and off the motor.

Like any other assembly being painted, part of the engine needs to be masked off, areas like the clutch and flywheel. The original cap and rotor are left in place for the cleaning and later the painting, as an easy means of masking off the distributor.

The paint being used on the engine is the same product, the same sealer-primer and the same basecoat-clearcoat system used on the sheet metal and the chassis. "People always think you have to use some kind of special paint on the engine because of the heat," says Greg, "but this engine will not get hot enough to effect the paint. The biggest thing is to clean them up. A real thorough cleaning is key to adhesion."

"For components like starters, we tape them up, have them sandblasted, then they go to the rebuilders where they are thoroughly cleaned as part of the overhaul process. You don't want to sandblast them after they've been rebuilt because no matter how carefully you tape them up, sand will find its way inside."

THE PAINT

Like the chassis, the engine paint needs to be applied from a variety of angles so the paint will cover all the uneven cast iron surfaces. "People think that the paint will wrap around a corner," says Greg, "but it won't. It's like the sun's rays, if you are on the shadow side there's no sunlight – and no paint. Painting an engine or chassis is almost the opposite of painting panels, where you want long straight passes."

The first coat of paint is the DTM tinted primer product, mixed 4-1-1 with activator and reducer. After two coats of sealer Greg applies two coats of basecoat, allowing the first coat to flash before applying the second.

The final coats of paint are the two clearcoats applied to give the paint job good durability, and of course, the nice gloss finish.

Mask off all the parts you don't want painted...

The first coat of paint is one heavy coat of DTM primer.

...then apply the wax and grease remover. Spray one heavy application and blow it dry in a downward motion towards the floor.

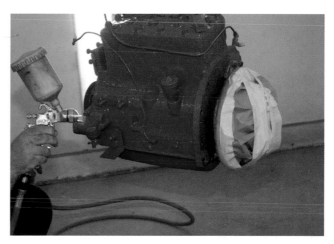

Be sure to get around all of the edges, fittings and lines.

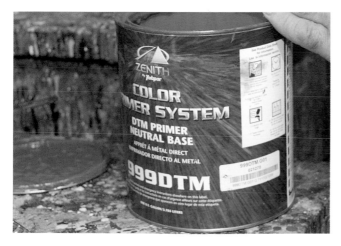

The primer/sealer being used is the DTM tintable product.

1 coat of sealer, 3 coats of color, and 3 coats of clear. It looks better than new.

IT ALL COMES TOGETHER
Final Assembly

Final assembly starts with the chassis. At this point all the subassemblies have been sent out and repaired as needed. The engine is rebuilt and placed back in the chassis. The kingpin bushings are new. Some tire rod ends, and all the rubbers, have been replaced with new parts.

This is when the organizing that you did (or didn't do) at the beginning of the project pays off. Painting and rebuilding Greg's tractor took a full 6 months, which is not uncommon. The point is, when you go to bolt the front axle, or gas tank, or radiator back in, you're not going to remember which bolts to use or where

The working days are over for this Massey-Harris Pony. From now on it's parade duty for this small member of the Massey family.

96

the funny bolt with the stepped shoulder goes. Which is why you put everything in plastic bags and boxes during the disassembly. And why you carefully attached labels and took all those digital photos.

If this is going to be a show-winning tractor then you should try to use only the correct hardware during the reassembly. In the case of the Pony, the hardware might be called "early American farm." Many of the nuts are four sided instead of six, and the slots in the screws are straight, never a phillips. This is another reason you organized all the parts into plastic bags, each with an identifying label.

Service and owners manuals are still available for many of the better known tractors and an evening spent searching on the web, or an afternoon searching the local tractor meet, is time well spent. Combined with the photos you took before and during the disassembly, a manual and a little common sense go a long way toward ensuring that things go back together the right way - the first time.

Speaking of time, it's important to keep the project moving along. Once you have it painted and any outside work completed, try to maintain momentum. If you did a complete disassembly as part of the paint job, the reassembly is a lot of work. Too often the job of putting it all back together gets stalled, until five or ten years have passed and your project becomes an embarrassing pile of parts in the back of the barn.

Set a deadline. A summer tractor show or 4th of July parade - and then don't give up until you're driving down Main Street throwing candy to the kids.

As with any engine installation, the key here is to properly center the clutch disc, so the transmission input shaft will slide into place as the engine is pushed up against the bell housing.

Greg was sure to paint all the engine parts. Nothing worse than finding out during the final assembly that one main component was never painted.

It's a very good idea to chase the threads on all the female holes. The tap will clean up damaged threads and also eliminate any paint residue.

At this point it looks like a tractor again...

Here you can see the starter bolted in place. The bolts screwed right into place because the threads in the casting were nice and clean.

...what's left is the sheet metal and a few additional parts.

It helps enormously if you can lay all the parts out on a bench. This makes it easy to do a logical assembly, and spot any missing parts.

The hood is held in place with these (original) simple hardware store bolts and large washers.

The finishing touch is the decals, here Greg determines exactly where they should be placed.

The film of water Greg put on the hood means he can move the decal slightly after it's placed. Once in position, Greg squeegees out the water and air bubbles.

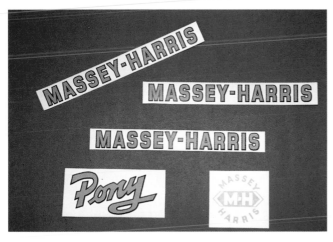

All of the original decals are still available. It's a good idea to let the paint cure for a week before applying the decals.

Once the decal has adhered to the hood Greg can carefully peel off the top layer, leaving only the decal itself.

Once he knows where they should be placed, Greg peels the decal off the backing material, and wipes down the hood with soapy water.

The finished tractor. A tremendous amount of work, but also a very satisfying project.

Chapter Eight

The Truck

From Flat Black to Turquoise

For the Truck part of this Tractor and Truck painting book, we started with a 1955 Chevy pickup belonging to Rick Thompson. We considered a variety of trucks before deciding on this particular example. Some of the volunteers were so rusty that the painting sequence was likely to turn into a rust removal seminar. On the other hand, we wanted to paint a truck that needed paint, an affordable truck, similar to something you could buy for less than a king's ransom.

Our finished 1955 Chevrolet pickup. The final color is 1957 Chevrolet Tropical Turquoise and India Ivory.

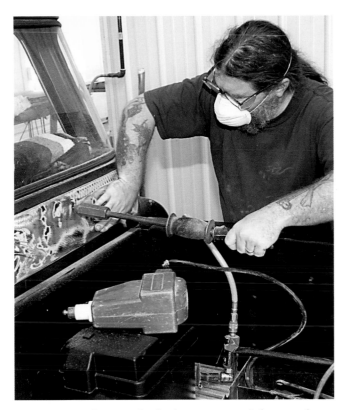

Bruce stops often to check the progress of the panel with his hand, it's easy to go too far.

spot and pull on that. What looks like a big gun is actually a small arc welder, the pins are steel, flash-coated with copper."

"The whole idea is to save work. People think using bondo is faster, but it isn't. And this way I won't have an excessive thickness of filler on the truck. Use your hand to determine how much is enough, you can always come back and put on another coat."

After welding on the copper-coated nails, Bruce pulls the area around the edges of the worst low spot, cuts the pins, grinds the center, adds pins to the center of the low spot and then pulls again. This illustrates Bruce's 'don't just pull from the center' theory.

"The trouble with the pins is you can go too far," says Bruce, "and then you have a mountain to deal with. You have to be careful too, to grind off the head of the pin, otherwise the heat-distressed metal around the pin will let loose later. The discolored, distressed metal is actually a skin coating and it will flake off later."

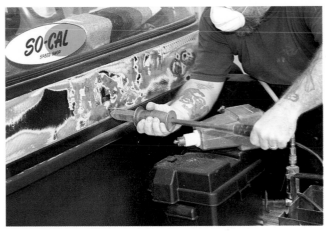

Working the shallow areas actually pulls on the deep areas, making the deep areas easier to pull later.

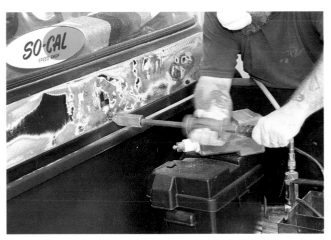

Don't be afraid to move from one nail to another and back again.

You have to be sure to totally eliminate the pins.

103

Slow and steady.

Now run the grinder flat across the panel again...

Patience is the key, you can't be in a hurry.

...the fact that the flat sanding disc takes off most of the paint shows just how far we've come.

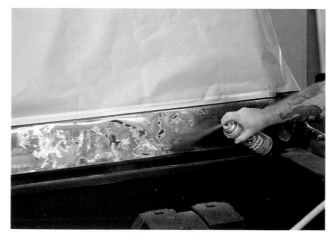

Spray on some flat black to act as a guide coat.

At this point the panel is almost ready for filler.

As delivered, the patch panel is bigger than necessary.

THE FIRST GUIDE COAT

Bruce uses this pattern of pins and careful pulling to eliminate the worst of the low spots on the panel. When the panel seems semi-flat, he applies the first guide coat (actually cheap flat black spray paint) and goes over the panel again with the big, flat sander.

The fact that the grinder takes most of the paint off the panel (note the before and after photos) means the metal finishing is done on this particular panel. In this case Bruce decides to go ahead and install a patch panel on the cab corner before coming back to do the filler work on this panel below the rear window.

A PATCH PANEL

A lot of trucks of this vintage have rotten cab corners and Rick's Chevy is no different. Bruce starts with an aftermarket cab corner and explains, "some guys would take the box off to do this, but I'm not going to. I will cut the panel down instead of using the whole piece." First, Bruce grinds the corner to see how rotten it is and how far up the panel the pin holes go.

continued, page 108

The cab corner, first you have to grind away the old paint and Bondo to see what you've got.

Test fit often.

A little trimming with a cut off wheel.

105

The tape makes it easy to cut a nice straight line.

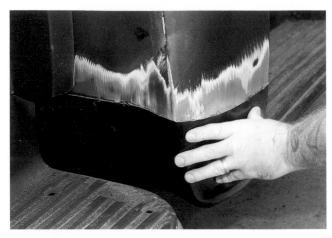

Now check that the fit is good so we get a near perfect butt weld.

Hold new section up and mark the edge with a felt tip.

After cleaning the edge of new section, the patch is clamped in place and and tack welded.

Notice how far away from hole we are cutting to get to "good" full-thickness steel.

Check the fit again, this is the last chance to adjust the fit.

Now we do a series of tack welds.

Grind the weld flat to smooth out the bead.

It's a good idea to work back and forth a little to keep heat and warpage to a minimum.

You have to grind off all high spots or they will stick out through the filler.

Bruce grinds and welds until the weld is solid across.

We aren't done yet, wire brush or sand blast all slag and discoloration off the weld or the filler won't stick.

I mix my filler on a piece of steel so none of the resins or oils are lost.

Here you can see the first coat of Duraglas...

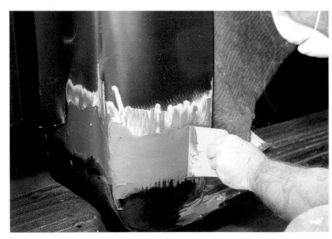

...applied with a flexible plastic paddle.

"Most people cut a big hole in the truck and then try to cut the patch to match," explains Bruce, "and that's the wrong way to do it. I keep trimming the patch until it fits the body pretty good and lays up against the body real nice. Then I mark the body where I'm going to cut it. I take my time and do a lot of test fitting before I start cutting and welding."

When he's finally ready Bruce cuts out the rotten cab corner with the cut-off wheel, leaving just a little extra metal at the edge. As Bruce explains, "Try to get it as close to a butt weld as possible, that's the best way. There are inner panels available too, but we're not going to use one here. If you do put in an inner corner you have to be sure to leave drain holes so moisture isn't trapped. Putting in cab corners like this is OK, but if the rust is too bad, just don't' do it, find another cab."

"Before I start welding I want to clean up the edges so they're' nice and neat. I can't stress enough the importance of cleaning the metal, It's about conducting electricity, you can't weld on a rusty edge. The clean-off wheels work really well, as does a wire brush. And remember that rust is a carcinogen so you have to protect yourself when you're grinding rust."

The welding is done with a Miller-Matic, wire-feed welder, set pretty low, about 60 amps. The wire is just regular 30 gauge wire, though they do make special, more malleable wire for welding sheet metal. The gas is an Argon and CO_2 mix, Bruce thinks it does a better job of shielding the arc and helps him avoid too much build up at the weld site.

Bruce takes a break in the welding and explains, "Heat is the enemy of straight sheet metal, when I weld I move around a lot. I don't weld in one area for too long which concentrates the heat. Moving around helps to minimize warpage and distortion."

After all the tack welds are filled in and the panel is fully welded on, Bruce goes over the seam with an air powered grinder and a 24 grit pad. Bruce also uses the edge of the cut-off

Next comes medium grade filler which works well on ground steel or sanded Duraglas.

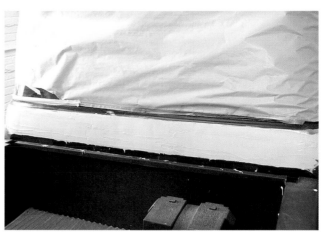

This method forms a thick, even skim coat.

Pull the filler...

36 grit works well for grinding off paint and rust....

...across the panel, spreading and pushing out the air bubbles.

...and filler, but you have to use this sander with a little restraint.

A 36 grit pad on a "Mud Hog" starts to get the panel in shape.

Here's the second coat of filler being applied to the cab corner.

Always work in skim coats to adjust surface evenly.

wheel as shown to "knock down the mountains." Next, he uses a wire wheel on the welded seam.

Filler Time

With a clean seam, Bruce gets ready to apply the first coat of mud. "Over the weld, for the initial coat of filler, I like fiberglass reinforced Duraglas because it's water proof and stronger than regular filler." Says Bruce. "For the rest of the work I use regular polyester filler or 'Bondo.'" I work in skin coats, if I can do it in one coat I will, but that rarely happens."

Mud the Back Panel

When he gets to the back panel, Bruce explains that filler should be applied to clean metal. "So with areas like this I grind the paint out of the low spots. I also grind all the bare metal fresh, because there's a layer of oxidation on the metal if it's been bare for a few days. And I like to feather the edges where bare metal hits the paint to minimize the edge."

"Even though it's more efficient to do all the grinding at one time and all the bondo at one time, I sometimes work in smaller areas and grind the filler, and finish one or two fenders before going onto the rest of the car," explains Bruce. "This is especially important for people working at home. I've seen so many cars that someone tore apart and then ground down to metal and then lost interest or they became overwhelmed. Then the parts get lost, and the metal re-rusts, and the owner never finishes. So in some situations it's better to do one fender or one area at a time. Do the patch work, the mud work and get it into primer and then move on to another area."

"On the first coat of bondo I like to let it set up fully, but after that I work the filler when it's still a little soft. With the Duraglas I'm not so worried about getting it perfectly flat 'cause I know I'm going to come back over it with a coat of filler."

For sanding the Filler on the back of the truck Bruce uses 36 grit paper on a 'mud hog,' which is just a fancy name for a large off-center air-powered sander. Pretty soon you can see some

Partially hardened filler can be worked with a cheese grater...

A sanding block works best for getting things straight.

...but as it sets up...

These AFS sanding blocks have rods that can be removed to create a more flexible block.

...it must be worked with the 36 grit mud hog.

Always block sand in an "X" pattern.

Back...and...

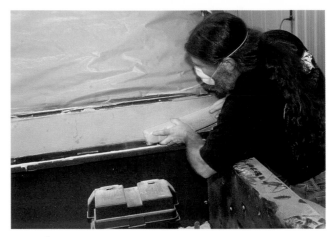

...and...

...forth...

....straighter.

...straighter...

Now we are at the "rough in" stage. Note the X pattern left in the mud.

Another application of filler, a finer filler this time, to the cab corner.

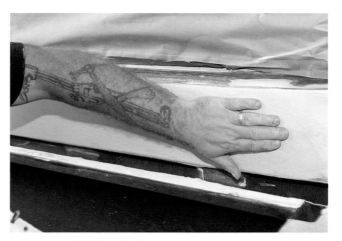

As you work, keep feeling and checking for waves.

Always mix per the directions on the can. And don't mix on cardboard, mix on piece of stainless or plastic.

Draw the mud through the hardener, so you pop as many air bubbles as you can. Mix until it is all the same color.

metal showing through (the high spots) and you can see the low spots the sander hasn't touched, so there is no point in going any farther. I will sand the low spots so all the surfaces are sanded, and then do a second skin coat of filler.

For smoothing the second coat Bruce uses the cheese grater, what he calls, "a poor man's mud hog," to trim off the mud on the back of the cab before it is fully set up. "You could do a whole car with just a cheese grater and sanding block, but you probably need at least one good power sanding tool."

BLOCK SANDING

After working the panel with the cheese grater, Bruce starts block sanding with 40 grit paper on an AFS block. These blocks are unique in that each one has three metal rods running through its length. You can take out none or one of the rods (note the photo) and thereby adjust the block's flexibility from stiff to semi-flexible. In this case, Bruce takes out two rods, explaining

The additional coasts of filler are put on thinner, and only where there's a remaining low spot.

Every step should get the panel straighter and smoother.

as he does, "I want the block to flex just a little bit. The mud hog left it pretty flat, but for more accuracy you want to use the block."

"I check the panel with my hand, my whole hand, and I can feel a few remaining low spots. We may have to fill small holes and grooves with spot putty, but that will come later."

"First I want to do another application of filler to the cab corner. I like to change fillers as I go along, so I end up with smoother filler as I get to the end. It also sands easier and doesn't leave as many pin holes. The other nice thing about changing grades of filler as you go through the project is that you can see when you sand through one layer and into the next."

Bruce decides the back panel needs a third application of filler, and explains, "At this point, I don't skin coat it, I just fill the low spots." After the third application of filler has mostly set up, Bruce goes back to sanding with 40 grit, the same grit he used during the last sanding done on this panel. Now the panel looks pretty good "I want to let this last application of filler get hard,"explains Bruce, "then I will sand the whole panel with 80 grit and see how it looks."

"As I block sand after the third application, the panel is shaping up nice. Once you've sanded with 80 or 180 it's much easier to feel the low

At this point I'm sanding the panel with 80 grit on a small sanding block.

Then finish up lightly with 180 grit.

Here's the 3rd coat of filler on the patch panel: One Duraglas and two applications of filler. Note how the round block fits the concave areas.

Always feel for waves and imperfections.

These semi-flexible sanding blocks are great for getting a contoured panel like this flat.

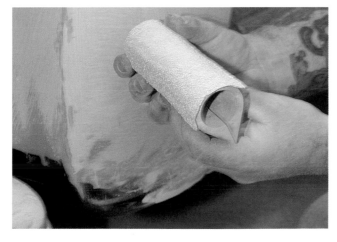

Note the round sanding block for sanding concave areas like the back side of the corner patch.

Feather the edges with a D.A. sander using 80 grit and then 180 grit.

115

Bruce wants to eliminate all the old flat black paint on this part of the body, to ensure that the new primer will stick.

Bruce likes Valspar's DTM primer system for its versatility and ease of use.

Tape carefully - primer goes everywhere!

Notice perfectly feather edged rings of color. Blow out all dust completely.

Newspaper can be used if you double it up.

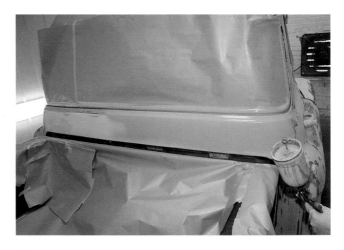

Then, prime away.

spots." Next Bruce works the panel with 150 grit on the long board all along the back of the cab and on the cab corner area.

PASSENGER SIDE SHEET METAL

Time now to start on the passenger side of the truck. "We just sanded the black paint off," says Bruce, "because I was afraid we would have some adhesion problems. On the cab I have to sand through the black paint to the cream color underneath, the black paint isn't sticking very well and I want to sand through the black to the paint underneath. On the box and rear fenders the black is black primer that was applied recently over good body work so I don't have to sand off all the black on the back of the body. The point is, you have to get down to something stable before starting the new paint job, whether that's an old paint job or the bare metal."

"And wherever there's a ding or dent you have to feather out the edges. For this part of the cab I start with the DA and an 80 grit sanding disc. The DA does a nice even job of sanding, and it has such a random sanding pattern that it smoothes those transitions, like where the filler meets the old paint. As you sand through the paint you should be able to see the layers like the rings on a tree. You want to be sure to feather out all those areas and edges. I start out sanding it with 80 grit and then end with 180 grit, the primer really sticks well to the 180."

"If money were no object I would have stripped this down to bare metal, but there's always a budget. Time spent on details pays dividends in direct proportion to the quality of the overall project, but you still have to know when to say when." Eventually the whole thing is sanded with either 150 or180 and it's time to blow it off, and start taping.

TAPING.

"I like to clean the rubber with lacquer thinner so the tape will stick," says Bruce. "And don't over stretch the tape or it will pull off later. I like to outline everything first, then go in with the paper. I often use newsprint, especially in the primer stage, but you have to use two layers."

Use an H.V.L.P. primer gun for high build.

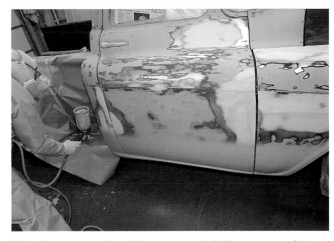

Use long passes just like you would if you were doing the finish painting.

Don't forget the details and the corners, and don't forget your safety gear!

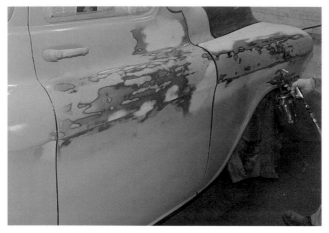

Bruce uses a 50% overlap on each pass of primer.

Here's the truck after 3 to 5 coats of primer.

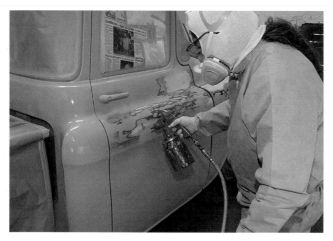

Pay special attention to repairs and filler areas.

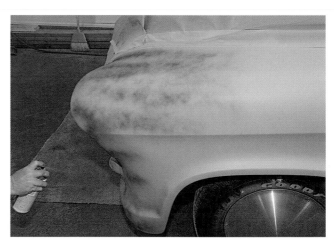

Apply a dust coat of flat back, a guide coat.

When the primer is wet you can see waves in the body work.

The guide coat will help you identify any low spots in the panels.

Bruce uses a squeegee to apply spot putty to a few small imperfections on the truck's right side.

PRIMER

The Primer Bruce uses is DTM Valspar direct-to-metal primer mixed with DTM 2000 #172 medium 75 to 85 degree reducer, "they have a great data sheet manual. This is tintable material so I had them make it up in grey to start with."

Bruce sprays the primer through a conventional spray gun (page 118). Note the way he lays the paint on in straight passes, with 50 percent overlap between passes.

"You want to put three to five coats of primer on," says Bruce. "Then wait 15 minutes between coats so it flashes, so it's dull looking, before putting on another coat." The paint I'm using is Valspar DTM 2000 primer surfacer, you can put this on bare metal including aluminum, and it is tintable. You can even put in extra thinner so it can be used as a sealer.

Use the same "X" pattern when you block your primer that you did for the filler.

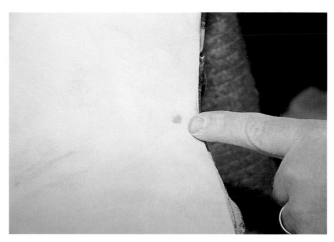

Flat black guide coat reveals a flaw in the body work.

Working the block until the flaws are gone.

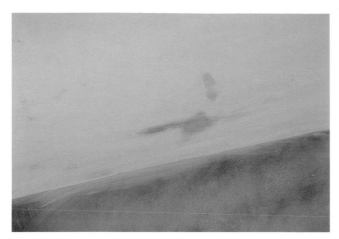

If you hit metal, stop and feel for flaws.

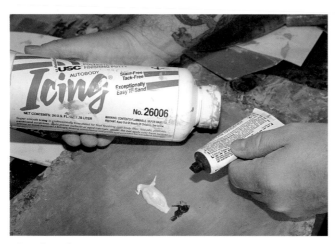

Catalyzed spot putty...

...is applied over small sanded imperfections.

GUIDE COATS AND BLOCKING SANDING

"At this stage 150 or 180 grit is what I like to use," says Bruce. "Most guys 'finish' with a DA and a 320 grit pad, and then they say it's ready for paint, but it's not really flat. The block sanding does a much better job of straightening things out, the more you block sand a panel the straighter it gets."

Bruce is a big believer in using a guide coat, "the guide coat will guide you by leaving a dark spot wherever there's a low spot. And when you sand through to the paint underneath, then stop, that's for the next coat of primer. This block sanding is the work part of bodywork."

Bruce sands using the same x-pattern demonstrated earlier, "in some areas you just have to sand by hand without a block. This is important, it's taking time and paying attention to details, that's all it is."

SPOT PUTTY

The little low areas like those seen on preceding pages should be filled with spot putty. As with any filler, it's important to follow the directions and mix it thoroughly. "This stuff dries fast and you have to be careful to put it on thin and neat," says Bruce. "If you put it on too thick you create a high spot and by the time you sand that spot down you've done too much sanding around the high spot so you've actually created a new low spot. Once the spot putty dries, just sand it with the same grit you were last using on that panel."

Bruce puts spot putty on a whole series of small low spots, "the spot putty should not be applied to large, unsanded areas because it won't adhere."

Below the door handle is a low spot, but before Bruce can sand off enough primer to eliminate the low spot, a high spot farther down pops out, and the high spot is metal which means there is no way to sand off enough material to make the low spot go away.

At the back of the door Bruce actually sanded down into the filler in order to eliminate the

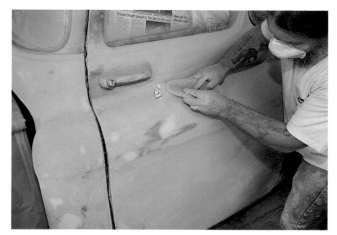

Block spot putty...

Retape and you're ready to prime again.

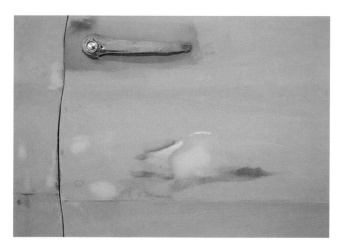

...first with 80 grit...

"I always use 3M tape, I've tried other brands and always end up going back. Always tape the seams and wrinkles as dust and dirt hides in them."

...then, 180 grit until all the guide coat is gone and the spot putty is smooth..

Now Bruce puts on three more coats of primer.

Prime even and smooth...

...just like you are applying the topcoat.

You may need to give a little extra primer on some spot-putty areas.

low spot that was there, "but that's ok because the filler was a little high there anyway."

After the door is sanded fully, it's time for more spot putty in areas like that below the door handle, as well as some other small areas on the door skin. Sanding the putty is done with the same grit used just before on the primer. "You could use 80 or 100 grit,"explains Bruce, "but that just gives you a deeper scratch to fill with the primer. Sometimes on a compound curve (like the bottom of the cab corner) the only thing that works is the palm of your hand." Eventually the door and back panel are spot puttied and finish sanded with 150 and left ready for more primer.

MORE PRIMER

At this point Bruce and Kelly have the cab block sanded and spot puttied, it's time now to mask off part of the truck, and then spray on another three coats of primer. Bruce explains that, "any areas that look questionable will get an additional coat or two. When you do multiple coats of primer, follow the directions. Be sure to let it dry adequately, this is really crucial, because the paint contains solvents and they need time to leave, and the material needs time to shrink down."

Bruce starts this next application of primer on the roof (page 121). "One thing I learned from Jon (Jon Kosmoski, founder of House of Kolor Paint) is that the primer is a chance to practice for the real paint job. When I apply primer I try to follow nice straight lines and paint it like a grid. I'm never sloppy when I apply the primer, I try to put it on as nice as I can.

DO AN INVENTORY

It's a good idea to take stock occasionally, and at this point the truck has come a long way. The entire cab is coated by two applications of primer. The Interior is painted. Bruce sanded the door jambs and hood jambs, and painted both in a multi-step sequence - first with Valspar one-step sealer, then with tropical turquoise basecoat, and finally with two coats of clear.

Wait until primer is flashed off dull before applying another coat.

Now we are final sanding with 320 grit. When we're done it should feel very smooth.

After 3 more coats it's very straight. Ready for another guide coat.

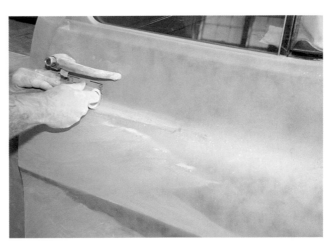

Contoured sanding blocks work for final sanding too.

Paint door jams and let the overspray act as a guide coat with the flat black.

Finally, sand small areas one at a time, blowing off dust. Check for flaws or waves as you work.

Bruce put 3M Rocker Schutz on the bottom because of its chip resistance.

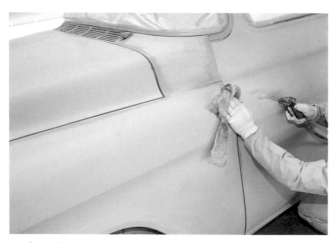

Before the sealer goes on, Bruce blows all the dust and debris off and wipes the truck down with a tack rag for a dust free finish.

The sealer is DTM from Valspar, tinted blue to make it easy to cover with the turquoise.

"The reason I do the jambs first," explains Bruce, "is so I can let the overspray just go where it will. If I did them last I would have to tape off the outside panels after they were painted, before I did the jambs."

The next job is to sand the outside again and then paint it with finish paint. The roof is going to be a different color than the rest of the body and Bruce starts there. Then he can mask the roof and apply paint to rest of the body.

Bruce does the final sanding on the body prior to application of finish paint, block sanding with 320 grit. Bruce explains that, "At this point the truck is pretty straight, so this final block sanding is really just a check of the work I did earlier."

To ensure he doesn't miss anything on this final sanding, Bruce coated the truck with a guide coat first. During this final block sanding Bruce does discover a few remaining low spots. "I can fix these with a little spot putty," explains Bruce. "Don't be afraid to back up a little during the job, you can add spot putty at almost any time, right up to the application of the final top-coats."

Other than the few small low areas already mentioned, all of the guide coat does disappear during the final block sanding, which means the truck is ready for final painting.

There is, however, one more thing to do before the basecoat and the clear go on.

CHIP GUARD

The chip guard Bruce applies is from 3M. "it acts as a cushion," explains Bruce, "and keeps the bottom edges from getting so chipped up. You can buy it in a spray can or buy it in quarts. One coat is good enough. I like to let it sit about 30 minutes, up to an hour, before I apply a topcoat. I thin it down more than they say because then it dries faster. I use the same reducer I use in the regular paint job, number 171 in this case, you can tint it too by just dumping some paint into the chip guard."

The sealer is applied in one nice even, wet coat.

Bruce paints the edges and corners first...

The sealer provides a high hiding, single color to paint over.

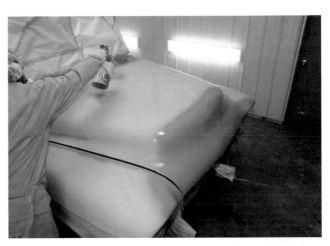

...and then fills in the big rectangle with grid-like passes.

Note that the sealer dries dull.

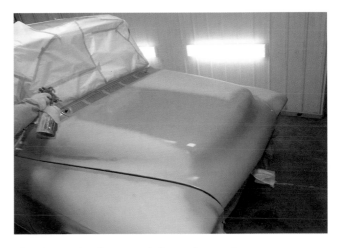

Again, notice how straight each pass is.

I seal all the paint surfaces to make everything the same color. The sealer also promotes adhesion of the topcoats.

Bruce uses a 50% overlap pattern for the sealer.

Let the sealer "flash off" until its good and dull (at least twenty minutes).

A shiny wet coat gives you a "last check" for straightness.

A TROPICAL TURQUOISE CHEVY TRUCK

Before the truck can become turquoise it needs to turn light blue first. That's because the Valspar DTM Zbase tintable sealer is tinted blue in this case. Bruce reduces the sealer with number 172 reducer. This product is very flexible and can be applied to bare metal as the first primer/sealer (it can even be sanded) or in situations like this it can be used as a sealer to be applied before the basecoat. This is actually the same product as the grey "primer" seen earlier, but with a different tint. We will do only 1 coat of sealer, reduced 4 parts sealer to 1 part activator and 2 parts reducer.

continued, page 130

Valspar's "Z Base" tropical turquoise. Careful measuring ensures consistency and less waste.

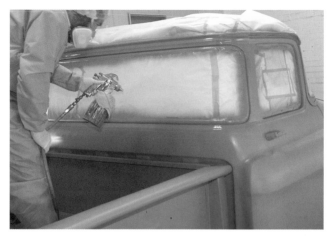

I also like to paint edges and crevices first.

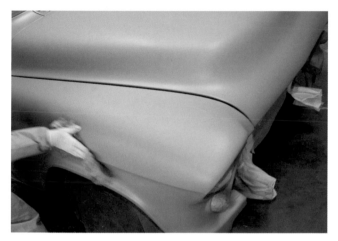

Bruce blows the truck off with 50 lbs. of air and wipes it down with a tack rag to remove any lint or dust.

I paint one end to the other without stopping.

I start with the inside of the box and the back of cab.

So as you go, you are melting in your overspray.

127

Outlining and painting tight areas...

In this case Bruce works his way around the window...

...ensures full coverage.

...before moving on to the rest of the side. Be sure to take your time and get everything.

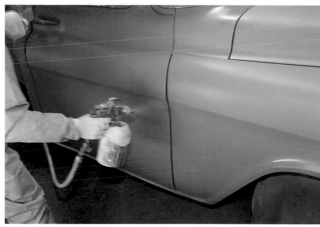

After the outlining is done Bruce starts to lay down long straight passes, done at a consistent speed and without pause...

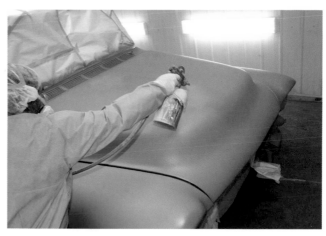

Painting the hood starts in the center...

...working up, pass by pass...

...and moves out...

...until one panel is completely covered.

...much the way the side was painted.

"Watch the reflection of the light in the paint...

Second and third coats require the same spray techniques.

...and how the project is taking the paint."

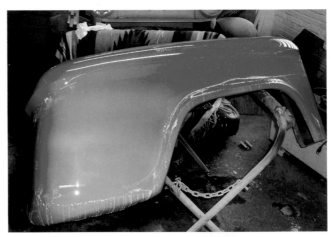

We pulled the rear fenders off earlier. Here they are after the buff ready to be cleaned and installed.

This is the truck after the full first coat.

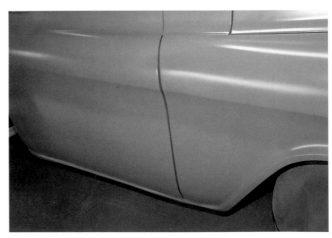

Here you can see the second coat going on.

By the third coat the paint really shines!

The finished truck complete with a white top. The white is applied in the same series of steps as the turquoise.

Q&A Bruce Bush

Bruce: How long have you been doing body and paint work?

Since 1976. My dad was a car nut, always went to the car shows, and always took me. I was fascinated and pretty soon I started hanging around at friend's dad's body shop. Before that I was building model cars, and customizing my bicycles. My mom has a picture of me doing a custom blend candy job on a bike in my backyard, I was 13. Ripon, Wisconsin, where I grew up, was a real motorhead town, we had a neat Main St, just like American Graffiti.

When did you open your first shop?

In 1982, I rented a two-car garage for fifty bucks a month. I built and painted custom cars, and painted lots of motorcycles. We used to do a lot of flames and a lot of hand-rubbed lacquer jobs. I painted everything I could in my hometown and then I moved to Minneapolis-St. Paul and opened a shop here.

Tell us a little about the type of work that comes through your shop?

The cars are all older than 1972, somehow that's my cutoff. And we still paint plenty of motorcycles.

When we were in the shop you talked about doing an inventory of the vehicle before the work starts. Can you talk more about this and about determining ahead of time how far you're going to go with a particular vehicle?

You have to create a plan, you need reasonable goals. Don't start with a rotten car and expect to build a show winner. Be reasonable in your expectations. And before you actually start on the car you have to look at every dent and every rust hole, circle them with a marker or put a piece of tape on each one. It helps you to plan and really understand the job you're taking on.

When it comes to painting and bodywork, what separates old trucks like the one we painted here from more modern vehicles?

The metal is thicker and more workable. You could say the metal is more pliable or malleable. You can do more with an old car or truck for that reason.

Does that make the bodywork more or less difficult?

It's less difficult. You can make mistakes, correct them and still get a good end result. These older vehicles are more forgiving,

They're easier to weld 'cause the metal is heavier and less prone to warpage. Some of the new cars are made of tin foil and you have to be really careful for that reason.

How do you approach rust?

It's a time thing. How much time will it take me to fix the rust versus the time and money for a clean panel. For example, you can buy a truck door for a Chevy truck pretty cheap so it doesn't pay to do rust repair. If you are repairing a tailgate on a Nomad, then you probably have to fix it because you can't buy a new one and probably can't find a good used one.

For a person working at home, do you recommend single or two-stage paint, and why?

For a truck like this I recommend two-stage paint. First, you don't catalyze the base coat (at least with the Valspar product). So you don't have to deal with isocyanates until you apply the clear. And with a basecoat/clearcoat paint job, it's easier to fix a dent in the new paint, it's easier to fix and blend a small area.

What are the most common mistakes made by first-time and non-professional painters?

First, they take on too big a project for their first job. Second, they put on too much material. Too much filler, too much primer and too much paint. Third, they don't read the directions, which is very important.

When you are doing a complete paint job, do you stay with one brand for all the paint materials?

Q&A Bruce Bush

Yes, I do. The primer, the basecoat and the clear all come form the same company. I know those products have chemical compatibility. I won't have any trouble with lifting paint or delamination.

What's required, what does a person need for a spray gun and compressor?

You need to have at least a five horsepower compressor. In terms of a gun, buy a good mid-grade, mid-price HVLP, gravity-feed gun. I don't think it makes sense to pay eight hundred dollars for a gun when you might only use it once or twice. All the brand name guns work, you just have to get used to the one you have.

When I started I borrowed some guns to try them and see what I liked. If you have a friend in the business, see if you can borrow a couple of guns and try them out before you buy a new one.

How about a shop, what is required for a shop and paint booth?

Really, you only need a two-car garage. That's plenty for your own project. George and Sam Barris started in a converted chicken coop.

Air movement is crucial. You are supposed to change the air every 15 minutes. A good fan is the most important part of the equipment. You have to have a good fan and you have to wear a good charcoal mask.

How do you deal with dust in a small shop?

Well, a lot of the dust actually comes off the vehicle, which is why it's important to blow the car off and wipe it down with a tack rag before you start. And your clothes contribute a great deal of dust as well, which is why it's such a good idea to wear a paint suit. Obviously it's a good idea to clean the booth ahead of time, and most guys like to wet down the floor so it traps and holds any dust. The fancier the paint job the more time you need to spend on every part of the process.

Talented, versatile and hard working, Bruce Bush will work on nearly anything, just as long as it isn't too new.

Chapter Nine

Powder Paint

Painting with Solids

There's more than one way to fix a problem and more than one way to apply paint. For machinery and industrial parts the process of powder coating is becoming more and more popular. Unlike liquid paint, powder paint is just that – powder.

The pulverized paint is placed in a small hopper, where air pressure feeds it to the gun. As the powder leaves the gun it picks up an electrical charge, and it is this difference in voltage

Nearly any metal part can be powder coated. Though these engine bits are boring black, a wide variety of colors are available, even custom mixes if you're coating enough stuff. As time goes on this process gets better and better, with a finish that often rivals that of liquid paint.

potential between the particles of paint and the part itself that causes the powder to drift onto the part. The powder isn't so much "sprayed" on the part as it is aimed at the part at close range. Once free of the gun, the powder drifts in a slow motion cloud up to, and onto, the part. After the part is coated with powder it is placed in the oven, where the bake cycle turns the solid to a liquid so it can attach itself to the metal parts.

The basic powder coat spray booth. The filters in the back capture all the "overspray" which is non-toxic and can be just dumped in the trash.

The best thing about powder paint is the super durable bond that occurs between the paint and the metal. For chassis parts or anything subjected to rough use, powder coat is the answer. A piece of sheet metal that's been powder coated can be bent into nearly any shape after painting and the paint stays right where it started. Chassis parts coated with powder are pretty much immune to rock chips and will still look new years after the paint is applied.

Another big advantage of powder paint is the very minimal amount of waste and the total lack of VOCs that are produced during the powder-painting process. There is no problem with toxic waste disposal or taking things to the county pick up site because there are no toxic products or even by-products of the process. The paint dust is just that, dust that can be swept up into a pan and dumped in the trash. Some powder shops take all the left over powder and bake it into an inert brick which, again, they simply dump legally into the trash.

What started as an industrial application known mostly for boring colors and rough texture, has evolved to the point where a good shop can match nearly any color, including candies

The powder starts out in this hopper, which connects to the gun.

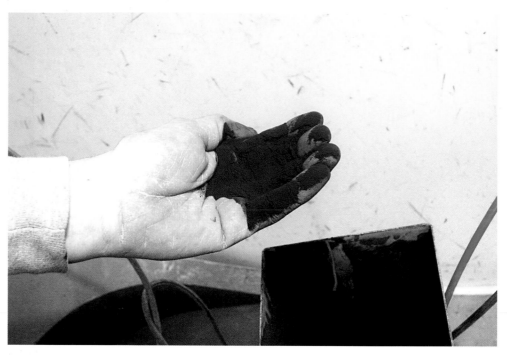

The material itself consists of very finely ground paint particles.

and clears. As far as the finish is concerned, there are two issues. One is the texture of the metal being coated. The other is the improving powder products. With a little care, a good powder shop can create a finished texture that rivals that of a good spray gun or liquid paint application.

Q&A: Troy Anderson, Premier Powder Coating

To provide a little insight into the process, we spent an afternoon with Troy Anderson at Premier Powder Coating in Princeton, Minnesota. What follows is a short interview with Troy, and a series of photos taken in his shop.

Troy, tell us, what can you and can't you powder coat?

We can powder coat almost any metal, including steel, aluminum, stainless and magnesium. Because it's an electro-static process, we can't do plastic, or metal parts with any Bondo or filler in them. The parts have to be one-hundred percent metal.

What's the best single thing about a powder coated surface?

The paint film is just so very durable. You just about can't get it off the parts even if you wanted to.

Air pressure moves the material from the hopper to the gun and then onto the part. The paint leaves the gun a cloud and drifts toward the piece.

138

Start to Finish Powder Coat

Troy starts with a motorcycle swingarm that's already been sandblasted.

After working his way around the component with the gun, all the surfaces are covered in powder...

Plugs like this are used to mask off holes where Troy doesn't want to have any paint.

...the next step is to the oven, where the high temperature turns the power to a liquid...

The powder leaves the gun as a soft mist, drawn to the part by difference in voltage between the paint and the part.

...which flows out and bonds tenaciously to the steel.

What is the best preparation for powder coating?

Sand blasting. I like to start with a part that's blasted to what they call a white finish, which is why we do most of our own blasting. You need a perfectly blasted surface so there is no moisture or rust in the bottom of the pits. If there's moisture, then when we heat the part to 400 degrees the moisture turns to steam and it out-gasses and leaves a pinhole in the powder coating.

What do you do with areas where you don't want powder?

We can mask those areas off with heat tape. Or we can use silicone plugs in threaded holes.

How about colors, can you match any color?

We can easily get the powder for colors like the John Deere and Caterpillar yellow. For a color that isn't so common we can do a custom mix. The only problem is we can't custom mix a small amount. We have to mix up a 50 pound box, so for some people that doesn't work.

What about the finish, some powdercoat finishes are a little rough?

Well, first, we often apply the powder to a rough, sandblasted surface, so some of that roughness comes through. To make the finish as nice as possible, we sometimes sand the blasted surface before we do any coating to eliminate some of the texture. We often do a second coat of powder and that really helps to create a nice smooth surface.

What is the powder actually made from?

It starts as liquid paint that they pour out and let dry. Next they grind that dry paint into a fine powder.

Then how is the "paint" applied?

We use a gun, it looks like an old timing

The John Deere is one of Troy's personal projects. In fact, he mixed up a yellow powder that is exactly the right color for the wheels.

light, to apply the powder. The gun puts a charge on the particles as they leave the tip and the part is grounded. So there is an electrical attraction between the paint and the part being painted. Even though there's an attraction, you still have to make sure the powder gets on all the surfaces and in all the creases and crevices.

And then the part goes into the oven?

Yes, the part goes into the oven and we heat it to 400 degrees so the powder turns to liquid and bonds with the metal. There is no dry time in the conventional sense, you just need time for the part to cool off.

Are some parts more difficult to coat than others?

Sometimes we have trouble with old, oily castings. The metal is somewhat porous so even if you clean it really well there may still be oil in the pores. In those situations I may bake it once before I apply any powder. That will help to drive out any moisture or oils in those pores. Then we let it cool, like I would any part that comes out of the oven. Then we kind of start over from the beginning, I apply the powder, and just bake it like I would any other part. The extra step really helps with oily parts.

The powder starts life as liquid paint, which then ends up in bags like these before being applied to the parts.

Troy likes to sand blast the parts that come in, because the preparation is such an important part of the overall job.

ADVANCED TATTOO ART

The art of the tattoo has emerged from the garage to the parlor, from the local bar to the board room. With interest in tattoos at a high point, the time is right for a detailed look at the art, and the artists, who create the elaborate designs.

Doug Mitchel takes the reader inside the shops of ten well-known and very experienced artists spread across the country. Both a how-to book and a photo-intense look at the world or tattoos, Advanced

Tattoo Art includes interviews with the artists that explain not only how they do what they do, but their personal preference for materials and methods.

Detailed photo sequences follow each artist through a tattoo project, from the customer's concept, through the sketch and outline, to the finished and colorful design. The chapters document not only the techniques, but also the inks and tools used during each step of the process.

| Ten Chapters | 144 Pages | $24.95 | Over 400 photos-100% color |

ADV CUSTOM MOTORCYCLE ASSEMBLY & FABRICATION

No longer content to build copies of stock motorcycles, today's builder wants a motorcycle that's longer, lower and sexier than anything approved by a factory design team.

Wolfgang was there at the very beginning of the trend with their Ultimate V-Twin Motorcycle book. Today they're back with their new book, Advanced Custom Motorcycle Assembly & Fabrication. Part

catalog, part service manual and part inspiration, this new book offers help with Planning the project, getting the right look and actually assembling that custom bike you've dreamed about for years.

Three start-to-finish sequences show not just how the best bikes are bolted together, but how the unique one-off gas tanks are shaped and then covered with candy brandywine paint.

| Nine Chapters | 144 Pages | $24.95 | Over 400 photos-100% color |

HOW-TO-PAINT BARNS AND BUILDINGS

The world is filled with wooden barns and metal buildings in need of paint. Though painting a barn might seem a simple thing the sheer size of the project can intimidate even the most die-hard do-it-yourselfer.

Painting a large building requires efficient preparation, the right products and some kind of spray application of the paint. How to Paint Barns & Buildings walks the reader through the easiest way

to prep the surface, which products work best on big surfaces, and the various spray equipment options – many of which can be rented rather than purchased.

To show how easy it can be to paint a barn or a building, this new book includes two start-to-finish paint jobs, one wooden barn and one metal building. Each sequence includes all the steps and illustrates how the right paint and equipment makes it easy to paint a barn or metal building.

| Nine Chapters | 144 Pages | $24.95 | 500 color images - 100% color |

BARRIS KUSTOM TECHNIQUES OF THE '50S VOL 4

Flames, Scallops, Paneling and Striping (Vol 4)
In this book George Barris explains how he and brother Sam did their custom painting and early flame jobs in the 1950s. No one can tell this story as well as George Barris, a fine photographer and the man who built many of the cars shown in the book.

People are as interesting in painting and customizing now, as they were when this material was first created, in the 1950s. Everyone wants to know

how to do a flame job, or how to run a pair of pinstripes straight down the side of their car.

This particular book contains more than just the photos and words of George Barris. This volume contains first-person side-bars by legendary painters and builders like Dean Jeffries and Larry Watson, describing how they developed their talents and what it was like to work directly with the Barris brothers.

| Six Chapters | 144 Pages | $24.95 | Over 300 classic black & white photos |

ADVANCED CUSTOM PAINTING TECHNIQUES

When it comes to custom painting, there is one name better known than all the others, and that name is Jon Kosmoski. Whether the project in your shop rides on two wheels or four, whether you're trying to do a simple kandy job or complex graphics, this how-to book from Jon Kosmoski is sure to answer your questions. Chapters one through three cover Shop Equipment, Gun Control and Paint Materials. Chapters four through seven get to the heart of the matter with complete start-to-finish painting sequences.

- Shop set up
- Gun Control
- Use of new paint materials
- 4 start-to-finish sequences
- Two wheels or four
- Simple or complex
- Kandy & Klear

| Seven Chapters | 144 Pages | $24.95 | Over 350 photos, 100% color |

PROFESSIONAL AIRBRUSH TECHNIQUES

Written by well-known Airbrush artist Vince Goodeve, this new book uses 144 pages and over 500 color images to explain a lifetime's worth of learning. Follow Vince through multiple photo sequences that explain his choice of color, sense of design, and preference for tools and materials. Early chapters explain shop set up and preparations of the metal canvas. Ten start-to-finish sequences walk the reader through Vince's airbrush work with both motorcycles and cars. Projects include simple graphics as well as complex and intricate designs. Accustomed to teaching, Vince uses a style that is easy to follow and understand. His enthusiasm for the airbrush comes through, making the text easy to follow. Vince Goodeve has something to say to all airbrush artists – whether beginner or advanced.

| Ten Chapters | 144 Pages | $24.95 | Over 400 color photos- 100% color |

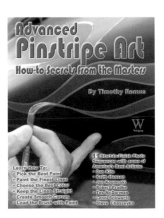

ADVANCED PINSTRIPE ART

Since the days of Von Dutch, hot rod and motorcycle enthusiasts have used pinstripes both as stand-alone art, and as a compliment to a flame or graphic paint job.

Timothy Remus uses color images to present the work of 11 well-known pinstripe artists. Each chapter presents one start-to-finish project and an interview with the artist. The photo sequences take the viewer from the initial sketch to the finished design. Text explains each step of the artwork, the interviews explain the artist's choice for paint and brushes. The artwork, often complimented with gold leaf or airbrush colors, is done on panels as well as various vehicles and components.

Look into the shop of some of this country's best pinstripe artists, for an intense and intimate how-to lesson. This is pinstripe school, taught by masters, brought to your own home or shop.

| Eleven Chapters | 144 Pages | $24.95 | Over 500 color photos- 100% color |

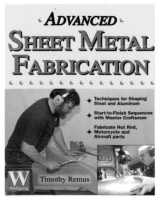

ADVANCED SHEET METAL FABRICATION

Advanced Sheet Metal Fabrication Techniques, is a photo-intensive, how-to book. See Craig Naff build a Rolls Royce fender, Rob Roehl create a motorcycle gas tank, Ron Covell form part of a quarter midget body, and Fay Butler shape an aircraft wheel fairing. Methods and tools include English wheel, power hammer, shrinkers and stretchers, and of course the hammer and dolly.

- Sequences in aluminum and steel
- Multi-piece projects
- Start to finish sequences
- From building the buck to shaping the steel
- Includes interviews with the metal shapers
- Automotive, motorcycle and aircraft

| 7 Chapters | 144 Pages | $24.95 | 144 pages, over 300 photos - 60% color |

Sources

Adjustable Flexibility Sanders
John Wheeler
Order: 877.459.7167
Tech: 651.459.7167
FAX: 651.459.7168
www.adjustflexsand.com

Anderson Implement
Reproduction Parts
31414 125th St.
Princeton, MN 55371
763-389-4275

Anderson Tire
31414 125th St.
Princeton, MN 55371
763-389-4275

DeVilbiss Spray Equipment
www.devilbiss.com

Eastwood
www.eastwood.com

Evercoat/Rage
www.evercoat.com

LNE Blasting
43528 Gladstone
Harris, MN 55032
651-674-5547

Northern Tool
www.northerntool.com

Premier Powder Coating
31521 125-1/2 St.
Princeton, MN 55371
763-389-4013
troy@premierpowdercoating.com

Redi-Strip
PO Box 72199
100 W Central Ave.
Roselle, IL 60172
630-529-2442
www.redistripco.com

Tractor Supply
www.tractorsupply.com

Tecor
Booths and Filters
14250 Judicial Rd
Burnsville MN 55306
www.tecor.com

Valspar
www.valsparrefinish.com

Wizard Paint
221 State Hwy 35
Centuria, WI 54824
763-238-2400